Appliqué Quilts

Appliqué has always been a way for quilters
to express their idea of beauty and form.
In *Appliqué Quilts*, you will find an exciting range
of projects including simple designs
for beginners as well as complex fabric pictures for
the more experienced quilt artists.

Whether it be Traditional Treasures, Bright and Beautiful,
Symphony of Flowers or Sweet Dreams, *Appliqué Quilts*
includes projects to delight everyone.
Wallhangings, cushions, miniature quilts, bed quilts
and even an appliqué table cover are featured
in this comprehensive book.

Appliqué Quilts provides beautiful colour photographs, clear
instructions and patterns. Machine appliqué, hand and
machine quilting, naive quilting and colourwash techniques
are included to delight and inspire every quilter.

Appliqué Quilts

VWM BS JY ccc

A Craftworld Book

Craftworld Books Pty Ltd
50 Silverwater Rd
Silverwater NSW 2128
Australia

First published by Craftworld Books Pty Ltd 1998

Managing Editor: Sue Aiken
Editor: Margaret Kelly
Associate Editor: Marnie McLean
Designer: Vivien Valk Design
Illustrator: Annette Tamone

National Library of Australia Cataloguing-in-publication data

Appliqué quilts

Includes index
1. Appliqué. 2. Appliqué–Patterns. 3. Quilting. 4.
Quilting–Patterns, I. Aiken, Sue (Series: Australian
country craft series).

746.445

Printed by KHL Printing Co. Pte Ltd, Singapore

Appliqué Quilts

Craftworld Books

Contents

Traditional Treasures

Bright & Beautiful

Symphony of Flowers

Sweet Dreams

Acknowledgments

LYNNE ALCHIN
Tall Poppies

Lynne Alchin attended classes at a patchwork shop in the Blue Mountains in New South Wales and when the shop came up for sale, she had to buy it. Lynne now teaches patchwork herself, with classes that provide something for everyone, from beginners to advanced. She believes that patchwork is only 'step by step' and it doesn't matter how long those steps take. Lynne loves vibrant colours which she has used to perfection in this beautiful, eye-catching quilt.

ANNETTE BLAKE
Fragrant Florals

Annette Blake's love of needlecraft has taken her down paths that she could never have imagined. When a leg injury forced her out of sport, she turned to craft, conducting classes at home. As the demand grew, Annette rented space where she taught patchwork and needlecraft. Her first quilt was a hand-patched wall-hanging and she has come a long way since then. Annette finds quilting therapeutic and enjoys teaching and bringing out the creativity in people.

CHRISTINE BOOK
50 Hearts for 50 Years of Marriage

A self-confessed fabricaholic, Christine Book loves rich country colours, but in particular, the 1930s fabrics with their clear pastel shades and cheerful quirky patterns. Chris teaches arts and crafts at a local school and the rest of her time is dedicated to designing and making projects. She designed this heart quilt which was made by her friend Kaye Harrison as a 50th Anniversary gift to her parents.

EILEEN CAMPBELL
Tu-whit, Tu-whoo Away with You

Eileen Campbell's superlative quilts are an exercise in perfection, with each quilt design developed totally in her mind. Eileen loves colour, and once the design is fixed, Eileen hunts for the main fabric which will fulfil the essence of the design. Her inspiration comes from nature, drawings and pictures. After experimenting with machine appliqué, Eileen decided that this was the method for her as she finds it quicker and more satisfying than sewing by hand.

JUDY CHRISTENSEN
Wild Rose Cushion

Judy Christensen enrolled in her first patchwork class in 1983 and has been a patchwork enthusiast ever since. Judy prefers to concentrate on both traditional and naive forms of patchwork. She has also attended many other classes, including embroidery classes. Her varied stitching talents can be seen in her collection of pieces which adorn her house at Glenorie, NSW. Judy worked with Sylvia Kennedy to create the beautiful 'Wild Rose'.

AILSA COWAN
Sunbonnet and Flowers
Floral Wreath Quilt

A country quilter at heart, Ailsa Cowan discovered a book on English piecing in a supermarket, which initiated her quilting addiction and jump-started a new career. Ailsa is also a teacher. Her classes include hand and machine piecing and appliqué, as well as machine quilting. Ailsa's ability to demonstrate to her pupils how to achieve their own unique variations on traditional quilting patterns is a quality that they cherish.

DONNA ELKINGTON
Fanfare

Donna Elkington began quilting in the 1970s when patchwork was very new to Australia. Donna's theory is that 'patchwork is the greatest thing given to modern women'. She lives and breathes patchwork and confesses that she is addicted to it. As a teacher, Donna's biggest rule to her students is 'don't follow any rules. Enjoy yourself! If something is hassling you, throw it in the bin.' Donna enjoys creating quilts of all shapes and sizes, from traditional pieced and appliquéd designs, to striking, contemporary quilts in vibrant colours.

YOLANDA GIFFORD
Simply Bright and Wonderful

Yolanda Gifford has four very artistic children. As sewing is no longer compulsory in schools, and Yolanda felt they should learn, she began teaching her children — boys and girls — quiltmaking at home. A friend's children joined in, then more and more, so Yolanda built a studio onto the back of the house where she takes school holiday classes. Yolanda is now teaching in schools, teaches adult classes and has travelled overseas, demonstrating her work.

LYNN HYLAND
The Three Little Kittens

The texture, homeliness and warmth of quilts originally drew Lynn Hyland to patchwork, but she has been designing for only four years. Although Lynn had envisaged a quilt on every bed, she finds that with small quilts, she can try out some of her many ideas. Lynn's designs, which feature unusual use of colour and strong texture, begin from a rough sketch, the spontaneity providing the final direction. Her designs are for the young at heart with a gollie, doll or bear applied to each quilt in the naive style.

ELIZABETH KENNEDY
A Quilter's Window Box

Sydney patchwork teacher, Elizabeth Kennedy not only inspires her students with her ideas and dynamic approach to needlecrafts, she is dedicated to learning as much as possible about her chosen crafts. Elizabeth has been involved with crafts since the early 1980s when she took lessons in cottage craft and patchwork. Teaching patchwork is Elizabeth's first love. There is nothing she enjoys more than fiddling with fabric, colour and design and encouraging her students to do the same.

SYLVIA KENNEDY
Wild Rose Cushion
Bridal Wreath Cushion

Sylvia Kennedy's love of patchwork began with a letterbox advertisement for patchwork classes. Later, she began teaching, inspiring her students with countless numbers of new projects. Sylvia prefers traditional quilts and finds colour the main challenge in her designs. She loves to quilt by hand but prefers machine piecing. Sylvia still works part time in a needlework shop, enjoying the contact with other craftspeople and keeping in touch with new products.

JANE MORGAN
Dresden Plate

When Jane Morgan opened a patchwork shop, she knew nothing about sewing, but her determination enabled her to acquire as much quilting knowledge as quickly as possible. She soon discovered her personal patchwork preferences and became a confirmed machine sewer. Quick quilts are Jane's specialty and while she engages in hand quilting, she prefers machine appliqué because she feels she lacks the time and patience to do appliqué by hand.

BETTY O'BRIEN
Serenity

Betty O'Brien started her first quilt in 1971 when she discovered a plastic hexagon template in an English magazine. During the early 1980s, Betty taught patchwork in a local craft shop. Her quilting ability is renowned and her creations hold pride of place in private collections throughout Australia as well as overseas. Betty photographs most of her work in progress to ensure the colour design creates a rhythm with the pattern over and back across the quilt.

TITA LEACH
It's Wash Day

Tita Leach was born in Germany where craft was compulsory at school, but it was not until she came to Australia in the 1970s that she became hooked on patchwork. Tita now teaches patchwork and the art of soft toys, combining both when she can. Tita prefers hand appliqué, embroidery and quilting because of the therapeutic benefit and closeness she derives from hand sewing.

VAL MEYERINK
Peonies Forever

Internationally known quilt maker Val Meyerink recently passed away but she will live forever in the quilts she has left. Val excelled at all aspects of quilt making but her true loves were hand appliqué and hand quilting. She was always keen to pass on her skills and took delight in encouraging others to excel in her beloved craft. Val will long be remembered for her beautiful quilts and her outstanding contribution to Australian quilt making.

VAL MOORE
Colourwash Heart Wreath

After watching a quilting demonstration, quilter Val Moore was instantly attracted to the craft and, soon after, formed a quilting group. Val began teaching in 1980 and later opened one of the first patchwork shops in Sydney. At a trade show in the USA, Val bought probably one of the first Baltimore quilts to arrive in Australia. With a team of quilters, Val conducts workshops throughout New South Wales, the highlight of which is an annual 'pilgrimage' to America.

CAROLINE PRICE
Sixty-Five Roses

Caroline Price's interest in patchwork began when she had her own fabric shop. She joined in the classes conducted there by the patchwork teacher. When she closed the shop, it was to concentrate on her growing love of patchwork. Caroline works mainly in pieced patchwork but is finding herself increasing drawn to appliqué and more contemporary work, as well as exploring all different areas of patchwork and quilting.

MARGARET SAMPSON
Penny Rugg
Antique Sampler Quilt

Margaret Sampson first discovered patchwork in the 1970s from the wives of American personnel at a military base. Through trial and error she taught herself to make patchwork cushions. Margaret's passion and skill for patchwork continued to grow and she was soon teaching. While Margaret loves pieced work, she particularly enjoys the freedom of appliqué. Her inspiration comes from many sources, which is evident in the naive antique charm of her quilts.

HILARY SMITH
Naive Appliqué Flannel Quilt

A lifelong passion for textiles and design has led Hilary Smith to quilting and, while she enjoys all types of quiltmaking, her preference is for hand piecing and hand quilting which she finds therapeutic. Most of her early work was in traditional designs and soft colours, but she now also enjoys naive and country designs in fabrics and flannels. Hilary also helps to teach aged people to sew as a form of diversion therapy.

KERRIE TAYLOR
Whirling Flowers Table Quilt

Kerrie Taylor has been quilting for many years and is well known from the patchwork shop which she used to operate on the New South Wales central coast, as well as the many classes and workshops she has conducted. Kerrie prefers the traditional or English method of appliqué and the bright pastels of reproduction 1930s fabric. She also loves to capture the feeling of old samplers with outline hand quilting.

RUTH VAN HAEFF
Dresden Plate

Ruth van Haeff first began quilting with her mother. She then did a sampler quilt on her own. Whilst working in the nursing profession, Ruth was constantly asked to show her workmates how to quilt. So what started as a hobby soon grew, and when a friend opened a shop, Ruth worked there with her. She is now working at the Village Quilt shop where she teaches all types of quilting. Her first love, however, is appliqué and hand quilting.

PAT WEIR-SMITH
Blue Bouquet
Chasing Butterflies

Miniature things have always delighted Pat Weir-Smith, but when she began quilting, she had no idea that her tiny needle and thread creations would lead to her reputation as one of the most prominent miniature quilters in Australia. Pat has also had several of her patterns published in American quilting magazines. Pat now teaches all styles of patchwork and holds one class per term in miniature quilts.

Introduction

Appliqué is an old French word that literally means to apply one piece of cloth to another in a decorative fashion. For nearly two thousand years, all around the world, appliqué was done by hand, using materials as diverse as leather and silk. Hand-sewn appliqué is still very popular today, although the invention of the sewing machine has brought about the development of elaborate embroidery and machine appliqué which is an exciting example of today's craft.

As quilters and quilt lovers, we all know that with some love and care and a measure of skill and dedication, little scraps and pieces of nothing can be pieced together to produce something beautiful. *Appliqué Quilts* takes

this skill one step further. We have gathered together a collection of beautiful appliqué projects from some of Australia's leading quilt makers which will inspire our first-time quilters to develop their own creativity, and the more difficult projects will provide a challenge to advanced quilters.

In *Appliqué Quilts* you will find easy-to-follow instructions, clearly set-out patterns and illustrations, beautiful colour photographs and a pull-out pattern sheet for those larger patterns which do not fit easily into a page size. Most of the patterns in the book, however, appear with each project.

Also included is a comprehensive list of the basic equipment required for

quilting, as well as the basic techniques used in quilting and appliqué. A glossary of quilting terms explains the meaning of the words and phrases that are used, and a conversion chart will help you with that precious fabric that is only 90cm wide. There is also a short profile of each of the talented quilters whose work is featured.

The projects are grouped into four sections: Traditional Treasures, Bright and Beautiful, Symphony of Flowers and Sweet Dreams.

SECTION 1: TRADITIONAL TREASURES

Included in this section are two cushions, a wall-hanging, and three quilts. These projects feature colourwash techniques, Broderie Perse, traditional hand appliqué and machine appliqué. Colourwash techniques and appliqué are used in the Colourwash Heart Wreath quilt. We'll show you how to make a double border and a lace-trimmed frill on the Wild Rose Cushion which is appliquéd on quilter's muslin. Blue Bouquet, a miniature quilt, is a flower portrait with fusible appliqué hearts and flowers outlined with tiny blanket stitches. Machine worked Broderie Perse is a feature of the magnificent Fanfare quilt. The Bridal Wreath cushion has a traditional appliqué design of hearts and leaves surrounded by elegant butterflies. There are two

heart-warming stories behind Sixty-Five Roses and 50 Hearts.

SECTION 2:
BRIGHT AND BEAUTIFUL

This section is made up of novelty naive-type projects. Instructions are given for two bed quilts, three wall-hangings and a miniature quilt. Simply Bright and Wonderful is an ideal first quilt with machine-pieced blocks, hand-appliquéd motifs, contrasting embroidery and hand quilting. Sunbonnet Sue and Overall Sam make a little quilt picture with fusible hand-appliqué techniques. Have fun with the Tu-whit, Tu-whoo wall-hanging using machine embroidery and quilting. The delightful Three Little Kittens miniature quilt features the Vliesofix appliqué method. Straight-stitch appliqué and Four-patch blocks are used in the naive It's Wash Day quilt. Add a country touch to Sunbonnet Sue with the Sunbonnet and Flowers wall-hanging.

SECTION 3:
SYMPHONY OF FLOWERS

For Section 3, we have chosen a variety of quilting projects which include a table

cover and the irresistible Tall Poppies. There are instructions for an appliquéd sawtooth border, yoyo flowers and puffed flowers; how to combine flannels and country cottons, and the wonderful world of Penny Ruggs using the freezer paper technique. The reverse appliqué design used in the Serenity quilt was adapted from a Rosemaling pattern, while traditional appliqué was used in the Whirling Flowers Table Quilt.

SECTION 4:
SWEET DREAMS

Transform your bedroom with any one of these magnificent quilts. You'll find an adaptation of the President's Wreath block and a perfect long-term project for hand piecing in Peonies Forever. Enjoy the age-old tradition of embroidery samplers in The Antique Sampler quilt. Use up your old-fashioned prints in Dresden Plate, with a pattern which involves both machine piecing and hand appliqué. Fragrant Florals will take your breath away with the appliquéd centre medallion which is surrounded by a quilted tone-on-tone background.

Now, take the phone off the hook and settle down to some serious quilting with this wonderful production of *Appliqué Quilts*.

METRIC/IMPERIAL MEASUREMENTS

Important

Fabric requirements are provided in both metric and imperial measures.

All fabric requirements are based on a minimum width of 115cm (45in).

The instructions for each project are provided in the measurements used by the quilter.

ENLARGING THE PATTERNS

Most patterns in this book need to be enlarged before use. To do this accurately, look for the photocopy symbol and number on the pattern (for example ▱ 130%), set the photocopier to the percentage given and photocopy each piece on this setting. Patterns that have the symbol ▱ SS (same size) do not need enlarging.

The History of Appliqué

The origins of quilting still remain unknown today, but history tells us that quilting, piecing and appliqué have been used for clothing and soft furnishings in diverse parts of the world since early times.

Quiltmaking is an art or skill that has always existed in some form or another, because quilts provide protection from the elements. As a work of art, they are easy to move around and many people find satisfaction in the use of interchanging different colours and different fabrics. Their usefulness has also contributed to their ongoing existence and the advantages of quilts include increased warmth, greater strength and the recycling of existing materials.

While it has gone in and out of fashion and taken on a number of forms and uses over the centuries, appliqué has always been a part of the quilter's means of expression of her idea of beauty and form.

From the early Middle Ages to the present day, appliqué was used in ecclesiastical embroidery. Gold work, traditionally associated with ecclesiastical embroidery and used as early as the tenth century, is really only appliqué.

The earliest examples of appliqué were made of leather and felt and were found frozen in tombs in Siberia. These have been dated about the 5th century BC. The craft was also known in ancient Egypt, appearing in painted tomb decorations. Whether it developed from the earliest times as simple patching of worn but still valuable items, or as a decorative art in its own right, we will never know, but it has flourished along with other forms of surface decoration of fabric.

As an ancient craft, appliqué, unlike patchwork, has almost always been seen as a decorative art. The technique of appliqué where one piece of fabric is secured on top of another has its origins in necessity, not in decoration. This evolved originally from the need to create patches to cover worn clothing. Appliqué-style patches were made from skins and hides. Now almost forgotten as a darning technique, the decorative function of appliqué has become an art form today although it has been regarded as a decorative embellishment for thousands of years.

After 1750, appliqué began appearing on quilts in America, where it was introduced by Dutch and English migrants. It is characterised by the album quilt, made up of different blocks, often by a variety of people, each of whom signed their name on their block. There was even a type of patchwork believed to have been devised from old flour sacks on the *Mayflower*, the ship which took pilgrims from England across the Atlantic. Cloth was at first scarce in the new country and pieces were reused, often more than once, leading to the development of traditional patchwork and appliqué designs. Patchwork then developed into a social activity in America with communities of women

helping each other to complete a quilt.

Appliqué patterns began to feature flowers and fruit in baskets, bouquets, wreaths and garlands. Baltimore album quilts display the appliqué style at its finest and an appliqué bedspread, worked on by a young woman for a best quilt, could take years to design and stitch. Many of these artistic quilts were recognised for their beauty and were reserved for display, rather than used on a bed, which is why many fine examples still survive today.

From simple naive appliqué quilts, other forms of appliqué emerged. Among these were Dresden Plate, crazy quilting and all forms of floral wreaths and baskets, vines and leaves. Many patterns were copied from old weather vanes, primitive hooked rugs and primitive paintings.

There is surprisingly little history of appliqué in Australia, although patchwork was well known enough from the earliest settlement. Perhaps there was a greater need of purely functional items and appliqué was seen more as a form of decorative needlework. Two of the main forms of appliqué popular in Australia are Broderie Perse and Baltimore.

In the seventeenth century, scarcity of chintz resulted in the evolution of Broderie Perse — a way of making a small amount of very expensive fabric go a very long way. The method used then and now is to cut out carefully around a motif of the desired size and apply it to a larger piece of fabric to form a completely new design. In Victorian times, the quilter was advised to use a thin solution of varnish for stiffening or a heavy flour starch paste. Both these methods were used to glue baste the motif to the background.

Today it is much easier to appliqué with the lightweight fusible interfacings now available. The stitch used was usually a buttonhole stitch, or the edge was turned under and hemmed with a matching thread. We can now also use fusible

webbing to glue the motif in place and neaten the edge with special paints. These paints add a pleasing decorative border to the motif and come in many colours including metallic finishes.

The other popular form of present day appliqué is the Baltimore style. These are outstanding examples of appliqué work and no doubt were never intended to be used on a bed. They were family heirlooms, passed down through the generations. Their value has been recognised by succeeding family members,

which accounts for the relatively large number which have survived in excellent condition to this day.

It was between the First and Second World Wars that quilts with simple country-style motifs became popular, with patterns being designed in America. While the traditional American-style quilt blocks still maintain popularity, there is an opportunity to develop a uniquely Australian style of quilt embellishment with simple, uncomplicated lines and naive characteristics.

Techniques

In the collection of quilt projects in this issue, each designer has her preferred method. However, you may find one of the following will achieve an equally satisfying result for you.

Basting
Turn raw edges under. Baste with a running stitch around the shape with a knotted light-coloured thread, beginning from the right side.

Machine turning line
Stitch around the pattern design outline using a matching thread and a small stitch. The stitched line can then be used as a guide for turning under the seam allowance.

Gathering stitch
Stitch around curved or rounded edges such as in a Dresden Plate. Place a light cardboard template on the wrong side of the fabric and pull the gathering stitch to fit the shape. Always press with a hot iron to set the seam allowance.

Fabric glue
Turn and glue the seam allowance on the wrong side of the fabric piece.

Fabric starch
Spray fabric to be used for appliqué. Iron flat, transfer design, add seam allowance and cut out. Place hard template on the back of the fabric, iron and finger-press edges around the template.

Fusible-webbing
Iron fusible webbing onto the back of the fabric. Trace design, add ¼in (6mm) seam allowance and cut out. Remove paper backing from the webbing. Carefully turn edges and press to webbing.

English template
Cut individual paper or light card templates the size of the finished piece and the fabric pieces with ¼in (6mm) seam allowance. Place the template behind the design, turn the edges under and tack them to the template. Stitch the designs in place. Remove paper templates from the back of the background fabric after the appliqué piece is complete, either by cutting a small opening, or by cutting the background away to within ¼in (6mm) seam allowance.

Freezer paper
Trace the pattern design without seam allowances onto the dull side of the freezer paper. There are three ways to apply the paper to the fabric:

Shiny side down on back: Position cut-out freezer paper template shiny side down on the wrong side of the fabric. Press with a hot iron to temporarily fuse the paper template. Cut out the appliqué piece adding ¼in (6mm) seam allowance. Fold the edge of the fabric over the freezer paper and press to get a sharp edge.

Shiny side down on top: Position cut-out freezer paper template shiny side down on the right side of the fabric. Press with a hot iron to temporarily fuse the paper template. Cut out the appliqué piece adding ¼in (6mm) seam allowance. Crease and fold the raw edge behind the design.

Shiny side up on back: Position cut-out freezer paper template shiny side up (a dab of fabric glue will hold it in place) on the wrong side of the pre-cut fabric. Fold raw edges to the shiny side of the freezer paper and carefully press edge with a hot iron to temporarily fuse the seam allowance. Position to background fabric and iron again to hold the piece in place for stitching.

Non-woven interfacing
Cut out the design from fabric, including ¼in (6mm) seam allowance and place it right side down on a piece of lightweight

interfacing. Stitch around the design outline, either with small hand stitches or
machine stitching.

Re-cut the interfaced design including
the ¼in (6mm) seam allowance. Cut a
small slit in the back of the interfacing
and turn the design right side out.
The raw edge turnings are now all inside
the design.

Preparing the background fabric

After choosing your background fabric,
you may wish to transfer the appliqué
design as a guide to placing the appliqué
pieces. Trace the design onto the right
side of the fabric with dressmaker's carbon, graphite paper or transfer carbon.

To see the lines clearly, use a light
box or tape the pattern onto a window
and trace using a water-erasable pen.
Some patterns may require enlarging
on a photocopier to appear full-size
for the project.

HAND STITCHING
THE APPLIQUE

To hand appliqué and not have your
stitches show is the goal of nearly
every appliquér. For handwork, the
hem stitch (also known as slip stitch)
or ladder stitch can be used to appliqué
the designs and used in combination
with the needle-turn method, will create
practically invisible stitching.

Blind hem stitch or slip stitch

This stitch comes up from underneath
the background fabric into the edge
of the design and back down into the
background fabric directly across from
the original point of entry. Turn the
needle so the stitch comes back out
again through the edge of the design.
The stitches underneath are diagonal.
The stitches on the top are parallel. The

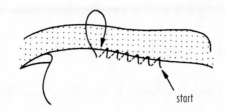

Blind Hem Stitch or Slip Stitch

length and distance between each stitch
should be equal (see Diagram).

Ladder stitch

This stitch comes up from underneath
the background fabric alongside the
design edge. It goes back down directly
opposite itself in the edge of the design.
Cross underneath the background fabric
and come up again, this time in the
edge of the design and going back
down again in the background. Continue
crossing underneath and coming up in
the design, alternating background and
design (see Diagram).

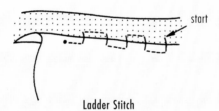

Ladder Stitch

Needle-turn appliqué

Prepare the design with added seam
allowance, clip inside the curves and
prepare the background fabric. Baste
the design to the background about
¼in (6mm) from raw edge. Insert the
needle at the back of the design, coming
out in the edge and going down into
the background fabric. Use the point of
the needle and your fingertips to turn
raw edges under just ahead of the
stitching (see Diagram).

Stitch from the right to the left
(counter-clockwise) if right-handed and
the left to the right (clockwise) if left-
handed. Space stitches equally apart.
Make the stitches even closer together at

corners and curves. Stitch up to points,
turn and sweep seam allowance under
with the top of the needle as you go, or
use a round wooden toothpick.

MACHINE STITCHING
THE APPLIQUE

For invisible machine work, use normal
matching thread in the bobbin and
monofilament thread on top. Smoke-
coloured thread should be used for dark
fabrics and clear for light.

Use a straight stitch to appliqué the
motif by stitching just inside the outline
of the piece. Then cover the stitching line
with a zigzag set close enough to create a
satin stitch finish.

Alternatively, set the machine to a
blind hem stitch and sew alongside the
design, positioning the needle so stitches
are placed just outside the edge of the
motif to give a near appearance. Placing a
sheet of unwaxed greaseproof paper
behind the background fabric when
stitching prevents the work stretching
and puckering.

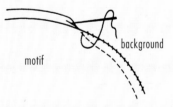

Needle-turn on outer curve – no need to clip the
seam allowance as it is being turned under.

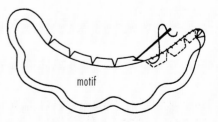

motif

Needle-turn on inner curve – clip the seam so it
lies flat under the edge.

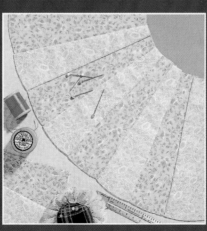

Traditional Treasures

There is something in a traditional quilt that invites us to pause for a moment.
Something that makes us want to stroke and feel the quilt — to absorb it
somehow — so that the quilt's thoughts and history can reach out to us.
Copy a traditional design or make an original work of art.
The treasures on the following pages will inspire you.

Colourwash Heart Wreath

*Colourwash techniques and appliqué
have been used creatively in the design of this delicate
and pretty wreath of roses,
which is the focal point of this charming quilt.*

It's a good idea to make a design wall and use a reducing glass for this design. A security door peep-hole makes an excellent reducing glass. It is inexpensive and can be purchased from hardware stores. Make the design wall from a piece of foam core, at least 110cm square. This is available from picture framers. The foam core is light and can be easily propped up. If you cover it in white flannelette, the fabric squares will stick to it, or you can pin them down.

PREPARATION

CUTTING

Make a window template by drawing and cutting an accurate 5.5cm square from cardboard. From this square, cut an accurate 4.5cm window. Use this template to cut your squares and to place a flower or part of a flower in a particular place.

NOTE: When cutting a large flower print, cut the square with the middle of the flower off-centre to get a better effect.

Use a quilter's ruler and rotary cutter to cut accurate 5.5cm squares on an allover flower print or tone-on-tone print.

A total of three hundred and twenty-three squares is required, but cut at least four hundred to give enough squares to 'play' with to achieve desired effects, or to trade with a friend.

PREPARATION

Sort the squares into the following piles:

- Squares that are mostly background with some leaves, tendrils, buds or vines. These squares will be placed around the outside of the heart design and also on the inside of the heart.
- Squares that are mostly leaves. These will also be placed toward the outer edges of the heart.

- Squares that have small flowers about 1cm round on them. These squares will be used as fillers in the design.
- Squares that have flowers about the size of a fifty cent piece. These will be scattered throughout the design.
- Squares cut from large flowers where only portions of the flower fit in the square. These will be placed to provide focal points in the design.

Referring to the design graph on page 22, start arranging the squares on the design wall, placing the squares as outlined. Now stand back and assess the wash effect using the reducing glass to check if any squares 'leap out at you'. There should be a gradual blending of the squares. Place the largest and most eye-catching bloom toward the bottom of the design.

CONSTRUCTION

Using a 5mm seam allowance, sew the squares together in rows. Press the seam allowances to one side by pressing the back of the work first. Press the front, checking for any pleats. Join the rows taking care to match the seams.

To make sure the wall-hanging will sit flat when finished, carefully measure the centre of the quilt from edge to edge, both horizontally and vertically, then measure the edges of the quilt. The edge measurements should be the same as the centre measurements. Make any adjustments required before cutting and adding the borders.

BORDERS

In this project, a narrow gold piping has been used between the quilt top and the border. A decorative uncorded piping could also be added to the edges of the quilt top. This should be done before attaching the borders.

Add twice the width of the finished border to the finished centre

FINISHED SIZE

- Finished quilt size is 105cm x 109.5cm (41³⁄₈in x 43¹⁄₄in).

MATERIALS

All quantities are based on 112cm wide fabric.

All fabrics should be 100 per cent cotton, prewashed and ironed. The background colour of the prints for this project is mostly cream, but some darker backgrounds can also be included. You will need a large collection of floral prints in the colours of your choice. The scale of the floral prints should include:

- Large scale flowers and leaves. (These can be cut and used to create larger blooms in an impressionist style.)
- Medium scale flowers and leaves
- Small scale flowers and leaves
- In the medium and small scale flower and leaf prints, include some open designs with trailing leaves, tendrils, buds and vines. The quantity of fabrics will vary according to individual designs – some scraps will require only one or two squares, while others will use most of a fat quarter.
- For the background around the heart design, 1m of cream tone-on tone print.
- For the appliquéd bow, use prints, solids or hand-dyed fabric. For the ribbon and bow you will need 20cm (¹⁄₄yd) of the main colour and a fat quarter of contrast colour. The rose buds are scraps of two shades of one colour. The leaves and calyx require three shades of green.
- For the border and binding you will need 1.2m (1³⁄₈yd) of fabric
- Rotary cutter and mat
- Metric quilter's ruler or square
- Cardboard
- Pencil
- Pins and general sewing supplies
- Sewing machine
- Cream coloured sewing thread
- Thread to match appliqué fabrics
- Freezer paper

Use the window template to cut the flower squares.

The appliquéd bow and rose buds in the centre of the wreath.

 HELPFUL HINT

Mitred Corners

Fold one border over another. Draw a straight line from the inner corner at a 45° angle. Reverse borders and repeat. Stitch borders together along marked lines. Press open. Trim away excess fabric.

measurements to allow for attaching with a mitred corner. From the width of the border fabric, cut two 13cm strips by the horizontal measurement plus 24cm and two 13cm strips by the vertical measurement plus 24cm for the borders.

Join the borders to the top of the quilt first, then join the borders to the bottom and sides of the quilt (see Basic Instructions). It is important to stop sewing 5mm in from each corner to allow for the mitres. Press the seams towards the borders, mitre the corners, trim the seams and press them open.

APPLIQUE

The ribbon, bow, leaves and buds are appliquéd. Trace the appliqué pieces 1 to 24 onto freezer paper and cut each piece out carefully on the pencil line. Iron the freezer paper templates onto the right side of the chosen fabrics. Cut around the freezer paper templates leaving a scant 5mm allowance. Clip the concave curves.

With the freezer paper template still in place, start the appliqué with piece number 1. Pin in place, referring to the picture for placement. Using a fine

Diagram 1

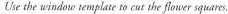

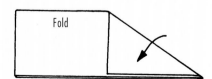

To make the buds cut a piece of fabric 5cm x 6cm. Fold the piece along the long side. Fold the upper right corner to the centre of the rectangle.

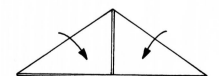

Fold the upper left corner of the rectangle to the centre.

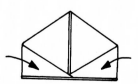

Fold the left and right corners of the triangle into the centre. Hold the folds with a pin, then secure with a few stitches across the bottom of the folds. Appliqué in place.

appliqué needle and matching thread, appliqué the ribbon in place by needle-turning the allowance using the edge of the freezer paper template as a guide. Remove the freezer paper template. Continue to add each appliqué piece in order through to 24.

The centres of the buds (18 and 21) are made of folded fabric (see Diagram 1).

QUILTING

Quilt the wreath itself with wavy lines reminiscent of twisting vines, then quilt random leaf shapes on the background around the inside and the outside of the wreath design.

The border is quilted with a traditional feather design.

FINISHING

BINDING

Cut four strips 5cm wide across the fabric width. Fold the strips in half lengthwise, press and attach to the front of the quilt. Turn to the back and stitch in place.

Label and date your quilt.

DESIGN GRAPH

76.5cm

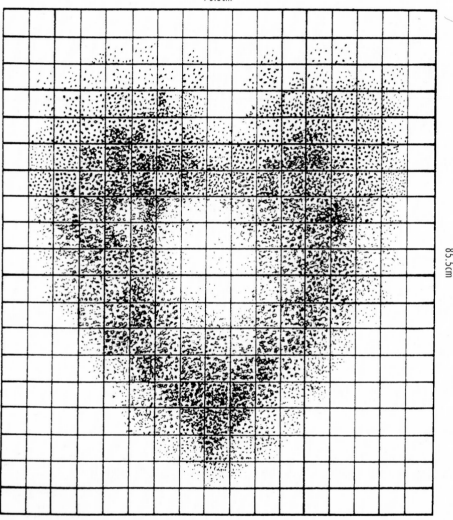

85.5cm

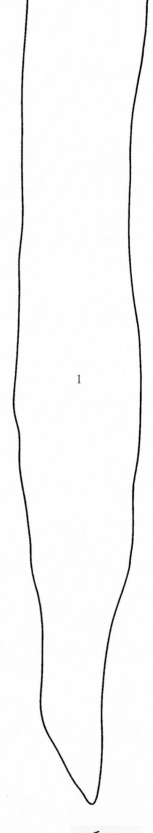

1

118%

APPLIQUE PIECES

118%

Wild Rose Cushion

This floral cushion, appliquéd in soft pinks and green on quilter's muslin,
is a variation of the traditional Rose of Sharon block.
The four-petalled roses have stylised curved stems, leaves and buds,
framed with a double border and lace-trimmed frill.

PREPARATION

Using the appliqué pattern provided on page 27, trace the pattern shapes onto template plastic and cut out the templates with paper scissors. Place the templates onto cardboard, trace around and cut cardboard shapes for each piece.

CUTTING AND BASTING APPLIQUE

Place the templates onto the wrong side of the fabrics you have selected and trace around each with a sharp pencil. Draw a ¼in seam allowance outside this line. This last line is the cutting line. Cut the shapes out of the fabrics.

You will need:
- Eight outer petals
- Eight inner petals
- Four buds
- Six stems (two of each size)
- Four leaves
- Two centres for flowers

CONSTRUCTION

❖

Baste the pieces of fabric to the cardboard shapes with the right side of the fabric on the outside. You will need to nick the fabric where there are concave curves and into the corners. Where there are sharp points, as on leaves and calyxes on stems, turn the point under first before the sides. Do not baste edges that fit under another shape. Leave these as raw edges to eliminate bulk. For the centres of flowers, make a gathering stitch between the pencil line and raw edge and gather up over the cardboard.

When you have finished the basting, press all the shapes with an iron to give a neat sharp edge.

FINISHED SIZE

- Finished cushion is 43cm (17in). Finished block size is 36cm (14in).

MATERIALS

All quantities are based on 44in (112cm) wide fabric.

- 50cm (⅝yd) fabric for background and back of cushion
- 10cm (⅛yd) of three colours for rose
- 10cm (⅛yd) of green fabric for leaves and stems
- 10cm (⅛yd) fabric for first border
- 70cm (¾yd) fabric for second border and frill
- 4.5m (5yd) of 2.5cm (1in) wide lace with edge to thread through ribbon
- 4.5m (5yd) of 2mm (1/16in) narrow ribbon to fit lace
- 50cm (⅝yd) of 5mm (3/16in) ribbon for bow
- 35cm (14in) zipper
- Template plastic
- Quilter's ¼in ruler
- No 9 Betweens quilting needle
- Quilting cotton
- Cardboard for shapes
- Threads to match fabrics for appliqué
- 46cm (18in) square of batting
- 46cm (18in) square of fabric for cushion backing (homespun or calico)
- 46cm (18in) cushion insert
- Sharp pencil

STITCHES USED

Gathering Stitch, Hem Stitch, French Knots

Baste the fabric pieces to the cardboard shapes.

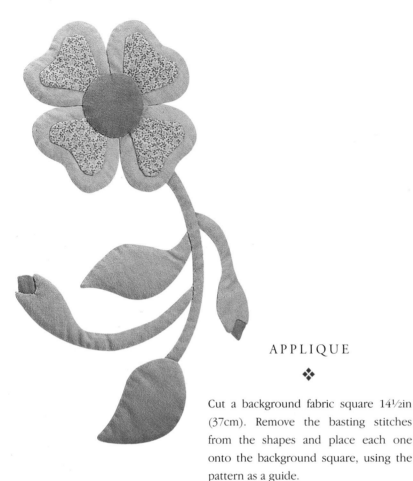

cushion top, batting and backing together starting from the centre and working out. Using a No 9 Betweens quilting needle and quilting thread, quilt the three layers together.

ASSEMBLING THE CUSHION

To make the frills, cut three strips of fabric 6½in x 44in (16.5cm x 112cm) wide. Join these strips together to form a circle. Fold in half, wrong sides together and press. Thread ribbon through the lace. Stitch the decorative edge of the lace to the frill at the folded edges, overlap and neatly join the folded edge.

Put two rows of gathering stitches around the frill at the raw edges.

Fold the frill into halves and then again into quarters. Place a thread or pin at these points, then gather up the frill to fit the cushion, matching corner points with the marked pin points. The half and quarter points will allow you to gather and fit the gathers evenly around the cushion.

Pin the frill to the cushion top, raw edges to raw edges, slightly rounding the corners. Stitch into position.

For the back, cut two pieces of fabric 18in x 10½in (46cm x 27cm). These measurements are slightly larger than needed. Join these together by inserting the zipper. Place it onto the cushion top, right sides together. Undo the zipper about 2in (5cm) so the cushion can be turned right side out. Pin it into position, then stitch, following the stitching line of the frill.

APPLIQUE

Cut a background fabric square 14½in (37cm). Remove the basting stitches from the shapes and place each one onto the background square, using the pattern as a guide.

Pin or baste each shape into position. Using the same colour thread as the fabrics, stitch each one into place with small hemming stitches.

BORDERS

Cut four lengths of fabric for the first border, 1in x 20in (2.5cm x 51cm). Cut another four lengths for the second border, 1½in x 20in (4cm x 51cm).

Join the first and second borders together, making four joined sections. Stitch the borders to the background square, mitring the corners. Trim away excess fabric. Press.

QUILTING

Mark in the quilting lines on the cushion top with a diagonal grid 1in (2.5cm) apart on the background. Baste the

FINISHING

Trim raw edges and neaten by zigzagging or overlocking. Turn right sides out. The bow in one corner is attached with French knots. Insert the cushion insert.

168%

Fanfare

*A variety of interesting machine stitches has been
used to construct this variation of a Grandmother's Fan.
Incorporating machine-worked Broderie Perse, you can also
substitute a beautiful lace if you prefer.*

PREPARATION

CUTTING

From the background fabric, cut twenty-four 12½in square blocks. Put eight of these to one side. The other sixteen will be made into fan blocks.

Using the fan block templates, cut sixty-four blades from the first plain fabric, sixty-four blades from the second plain fabric and using the fan centre template, cut sixteen fan centres from the third plain fabric.

Cut four 10in wide strips from the length of the border fabric.

CONSTRUCTION

PIECING

Make sixteen fans, each with eight blades of alternating colours. Make eight starting with the first colour at the top and eight starting with the second colour. Press the seams in one direction.

APPLIQUE AND EMBROIDERY

With the right side of the background fabric facing upward, pin the fan sections securely to the bottom right corner of the sixteen background blocks.

Securely pin the fan centre (colour three) onto the block over the base of the fan section.

Using a twin needle and coordinating embroidery threads, choose an embroidery stitch to cover the raw edges of the base and fan (we used stitch No 146 + twin needle key on a Pfaff sewing machine). If your machine does not do embroidery, some of the overlocking stitches in the machine will cover the raw edges.

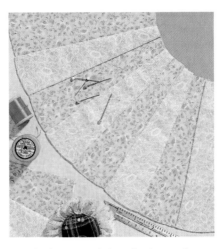

Pin the fan centre (colour three) onto the block over the base of the fan section.

NOTE: Always check the stitch width before sewing to ensure you do not break your twin needle. Sew across the raw edges at the top of the fan and at the fan centre.

You may also like to select a scallop stitch and stitch across the top of the fan blades.

NOTE: Remember to use Vliesofix under the blocks when embroidering to keep the work from distorting and stretching. Use ordinary thread in the bobbin of the machine.

Alternatively, the raw edges can be covered with lace. Attach the lace using a zigzag stitch with monofilament thread in the top of the machine. For those who enjoy hand stitching, traditional methods of hand appliqué can also be used to attach the fans.

Lay the blocks out following the layout diagram provided. Using a ¼in seam, join the blocks into rows, then join the rows together.

BORDER

Attach the outside borders to the quilt, mitring the corners.

Iron Vliesofix to the back of the extra border print, then cut a number of floral arrangements from the piece of

FINISHED SIZE

- Finished quilt size is 203cm x 152cm (80in x 60in) approximately.

MATERIALS

Requirements are based on 112cm (45in) wide fabric.

- 3m (3⅜yd) background fabric
- 60cm (⅔yd) plain fabric for first colour of fan blades
- 60cm (⅔yd) plain fabric for second colour of fan blades
- 20cm (¼yd) plain fabric for fan centres
- 2.5m (2⅞yd) border fabric, large print
- 25cm (⅓yd) border fabric for appliqués
- 50cm (⅝yd) binding fabric
- 2 reels machine embroidery thread to complement quilt colours
- 1 reel monofilament thread
- 1 x 1.6mm twin needle for sewing machine
- 50cm (⅝yd) Vliesofix
- 10m (11⅓yd) cotton lace (optional, see note)
- 5m (5½yd) backing fabric
- 160cm x 210cm (63in x 83in) piece of batting

NOTE: The lace can be used as an alternative to machine embroidery to cover the raw edges of the fan.

STITCHES USED

Scallop Stitch, Zigzag Stitch, Slip Stitch

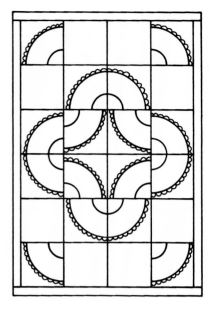

Layout Diagram

QUILTING

Join the backing fabric to make an 85in x 65in piece. Sandwich the backing, batting and top and pin or baste in place.

The featured quilt is quilted in the ditch around each fan blade and stipple quilted over the background. The floral design on the borders is outline stitched.

FINISHING

BINDING

Cut seven 2½in strips across the width of the binding fabric. Join the strips on the diagonal into one length. Press in half lengthwise, right sides together. With raw edges together, attach the binding to the front, mitring the corners. Join the ends on the diagonal, turn and slip stitch to the back.

Make a label for the back and sign and date your quilt.

fabric. Arrange the flowers across the quilt, either using the photograph as a guide, or if you prefer, position the flowers to make your own individual arrangement. When you are pleased with the result, peel the paper away from the back of the appliqués and iron them in place.

Using monofilament thread and an appliqué stitch from your sewing machine, sew around the appliqué pieces to secure them to the quilt top. Use ordinary machine embroidery thread in the bobbin of the machine.

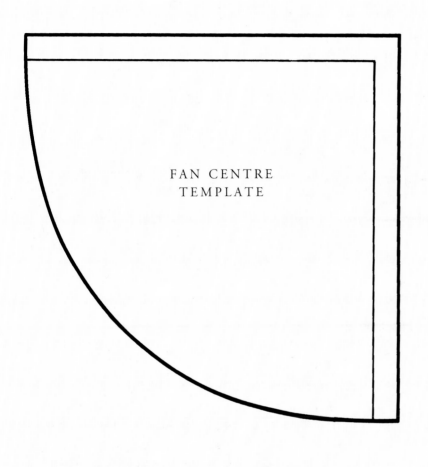

FAN CENTRE
TEMPLATE

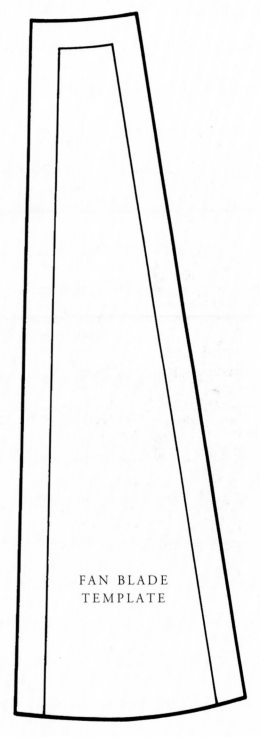

FAN BLADE
TEMPLATE

SS

Blue Bouquet

As delicate as a Wedgwood plate, this miniature appliqué
is a flower portrait in subtle shades of blue.
The fusible appliqué hearts and flowers are outlined
with tiny blanket stitches.

PREPARATION

CUTTING

From the background fabric, cut the following pieces:

For the centre, cut one 9in x 11¾in rectangle (you may like to cut this a little larger than needed, then cut down to the required size when you have finished the appliqué.)

For the main border, cut two 3in x 17in lengths for the top and bottom and two 3in x 20in lengths for the sides.

From the overlay fabric, cut one 9in x 11¾in rectangle.

From the fabric for the inner border, cut two 1in x 10in lengths and two 1in x 13in lengths (these are cut longer than required).

From the same fabric, for the binding, cut four 2in wide strips on the bias. You will require a length of at least 70in.

CONSTRUCTION

Fold the centre background rectangle in half both ways and finger-crease. Place this rectangle over the bouquet pattern and align the creases with the centre markings.

Using an HB pencil, lightly mark the flowers, leaves and buds inside the design lines so they will be covered by the appliqué pieces. Mark a single line for each of the stems.

The border design is easier to mark after the border lengths are sewn to the central design area.

When the borders are sewn, lay each corner section over the pattern and trace all the markings. The pattern must be reversed (turned over) to draw two of the corners.

Align the corner over the pattern provided on the Pattern Sheet and trace the markings in as before.

HELPFUL HINT

Turn the pattern over and tape it to a window or light box.

APPLIQUE

Using the given shapes, trace the required number of flowers, tulips, buds and leaves on the paper side of the fusible webbing.

Allow some space between the groups of flowers and other items which will require different fabrics. Cut out groups of traced shapes of each chosen fabric. Do not cut out individual shapes but leave them as a group on the webbing.

Using a medium-to-hot dry iron, press the fusible webbing (paper side up) to the wrong side of the chosen fabric. The traced shapes can now be cut out exactly on the drawn lines. Use very sharp, small scissors and handle the fabric carefully to avoid fraying edges.

Peel the paper backing from the shape and position it on the background. Some flowers and leaves will overlap, so they should be positioned at the same time. Work with about six pieces at a time. When the first pieces are accurately placed, iron them onto the background and blanket stitch around all of the shapes. When these are complete, iron another group of shapes into position and blanket stitch.

For the blanket stitch, use one strand of matching embroidery thread approximately 15in long. Start with a tiny knot on the wrong side and bring the needle up on the edge of the shape to be stitched.

FINISHED SIZE

- Finished quilt size is 37cm x 43cm (14½in x 17in).

MATERIALS

- 30cm (⅓yd) background fabric
- 30cm (⅓yd) overlay fabric
- 40cm (½yd) inner border, appliqué and binding
- 45cm (½yd) main border
- Scraps of fabric for appliqué, (three blues and one green) or your choice
- Stranded embroidery threads to match all appliqué fabrics
- Green stranded embroidery thread for stems
- Lightweight, paper-backed fusible webbing
- No 10 needle for appliqué
- HB pencil
- 50cm x 3cm (⅝yd x 1¼in) wire-edged ribbon for bow
- 1.1m x 10mm (1¼yd x ⅜in) wide fine cotton lace
- 50cm x 41cm (⅝yd x 16in) batting and backing
- Sharp, small scissors
- Quilter's ¼in ruler

NOTE: Sew with ¼in (6mm) seam allowance throughout.

STITCHES USED

Chain Stitch, Blanket Stitch,
Slip Stitch, Back Stitch

CENTRE BOUQUET

Chain stitch all stems, extending the ends a stitch or two under a flower, leaf or bud.

The stems above the bow are worked in one strand of green embroidery thread while the four stems below the bow are worked with two strands.

Position the shapes and blanket stitch them commencing with the centre group of five leaves and two round flowers. Continue to place and sew groups until the bouquet is complete. Press the work frequently on the wrong side.

CENTRE OVERLAY

Finger-press the fabric rectangle both ways and lay it over the oval design. Lightly trace the oval. Cut out the centre oval leaving ¼in seam allowance inside the drawn line.

Centre Bouquet and Overlay.

Snip into the ¼in seam allowance about two-thirds of the way. Baste under this seam all around the oval.

Place the centre overlay over the background and baste the two layers together. (The bouquet should be centred in the oval cut-out.) Using a small slip stitch, sew around the oval shape to attach it to the appliquéd background.

INNER BORDER

Sew the pre-cut 13in lengths to the sides, stitching through the two layers (background and overlay). Press away from the centre and trim the ends.

Sew the pre-cut 10in lengths to the top and bottom, press and trim the ends. Now trim this border back to ½in wide on all sides.

MAIN BORDER

When sewing the border lengths to the central section, centre each length. With right sides together, sew one border strip to the central block, starting and stopping ¼in from each end of the main block. Do not cut off the excess fabric. Add the remaining three border sections.

To mitre the corners, fold the quilt diagonally from the corner. Take time to straighten the borders. Pin the seams and borders together so everything matches and lies flat. Place a quilter's ruler exactly on the diagonal fold of the block and continue a line across the border section. Double check that everything is flat and straight before drawing the line. Clearly mark this sewing line.

To start sewing, move the seams out of the way, as there should be no seams caught in this sewing line.

Sew carefully along the line, remembering not to catch any seam allowance. When this is sewn, remove the pins and check that the borders and quilt sit flat. If all is well, trim the excess border fabric back to ¼in seam allowance. Press this seam open. Repeat this process on each corner of the quilt.

Trace the border design onto the fabric. Work on half of one side at a time. Chain stitch the main stem with two strands and the bud stems with one strand. Position and iron the flowers, leaves and buds on one section at a time. Complete the blanket stitching before moving on to another section.

Complete all the borders, then add the hearts and tendrils. Draw the tendrils lightly with an HB pencil where they are required to give a balanced design. Use one strand of embroidery thread and back stitch the tendrils.

QUILTING AND LACE

Sandwich the quilt top, batting and backing. Baste the layers together to form a grid of basting over the quilt. Quilt by hand or machine from the centre of the quilt and work outwards in a methodical way. This quilt features a ¾in diamond grid pattern on the overlay and the oval is highlighted with a line of stitching ¼in inside the central bouquet section. When these sections are quilted, add the lace.

LACE BORDER

Baste the lace into position inside and right next to the inner border. Begin in one corner and mitre each corner of lace.

When you have returned to the start of the lace, trim the end and turn the lace under at a 45 degree angle to give the appearance of a mitred corner. This can then be machine sewn on the edge of the lace next to the inner border. Hand stitch each mitred lace corner. If you wish, you can hand stitch the inside edge of the lace down to the quilt.

Continue quilting the main border of the little quilt in a random design around the appliquéd flowers and stems.

Before adding the binding, trim off the excess batting and backing.

Gently curve the corners. Make a template for a gentle curve and mark each corner, then trim.

FINISHING

BINDING

Join the lengths of binding together and press in half along the length of the strip.

Leaving a 2in tail, commence sewing halfway along one side, the raw edges of the binding aligning with the raw edges on the right side of the quilt. Ease the binding around each curved corner taking care not to pull the binding tight. When you have sewn right around the quilt and returned to the starting point, stop sewing approximately 2in from the start of the tail. Remove the quilt from the machine and take the time to pin and join the ends carefully. To do this, trim the excess binding and insert into the beginning tail which has a turned-in seam. Sew this final section.

Turn the binding to the back of the quilt and slip stitch down by hand.

With the wire-edged ribbon, tie a small ribbon bow and carefully attach it to the central bouquet. A few stitches behind the central knot is sufficient.

Because appliqué quilts have such a lot of time invested in them, it is important to document all the information about your quilt onto a piece of fabric, using a permanent marker pen or a needle and thread. Slip stitch the label to the back of the quilt.

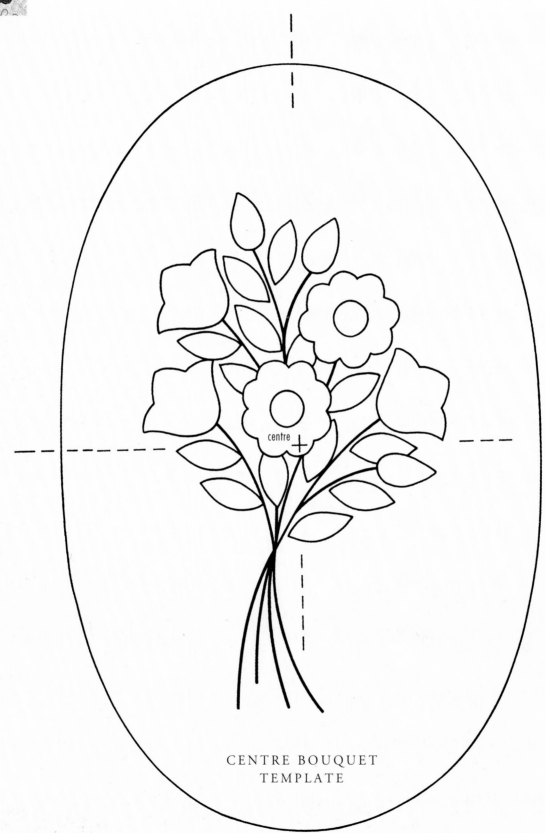

centre

CENTRE BOUQUET
TEMPLATE

Sixty-Five Roses

Inspiration for this beautiful machine-appliquéd quilt
came from the poignant story of a young girl suffering from cystic fibrosis.
When the girl's little brother was asked what was wrong with his sister,
he simply replied that she had '65 roses'.

FINISHED SIZE

- Finished quilt size is 155cm x 210cm (61in x 83in).

MATERIALS

- 2.4m (2¾yd) of white damask 180cm (71in) wide for background
- Fat quarters of seven or eight green fabrics
- Small scraps of at least twenty different greens for leaves and calyxes
- 65, 10cm (4in) squares of light to deep pink fabrics (at least twenty different ones to give quilt depth)
- Fat quarter of dusty pink fabric for first ribbon
- Fat quarter of deep burgundy fabric for second ribbon
- Sufficient batting to fit
- 2.4m (2¾yd) of 180cm (71in) wide white damask for backing
- 40cm (⅜yd) of 180cm (71in) wide white damask for binding
- Freezer paper
- Thin cardboard (eg manilla folder)
- Template plastic
- ½in (12mm) bias press bar
- Open-toe appliqué foot
- Tweezers
- White thread for bobbin
- Quilting and monofilament thread
- Rotary cutter, mat and ruler
- Sewing machine
- 2B pencil
- Seam ripper or Tailor's awl

NOTE: All fabrics are pre-washed and ironed. This is particularly important with the damask because of its shrinkage rate.

STITCHES USED

Blind Hem Stitch, Back Stitch,

Herringbone Stitch

This quilt is dedicated to Caroline Price's special friend, Michelle, who lost her battle and to those young people who continue to fight this dreadful disease. Caroline hopes it may inspire you to make your own Sixty-Five Roses quilt to raise much-needed funds for your local cystic fibrosis association.

PREPARATION

Follow the instructions on the appliqué pattern to increase the size of the pieces. Trace the pattern onto white damask using a light pencil mark. Keep the tracing to the inside of the lines so that the appliqué will cover them. It is not necessary to mark the bud outlines.

The base of the heart wreath is approximately 33½in (85cm) from the lower edge of the damask. The knot on the corner bunches of roses is approximately 10½in (27cm) from the side and lower edge of the fabric as detailed on the Pattern Sheet.

Trace the calyx and leaf patterns onto template plastic. Cut them out carefully.

CONSTRUCTION

BLIND HEM STITCH APPLIQUE

Set the machine to blind hem stitch with a much-reduced width and length. On a Bernina sewing machine, the stitch width is 1 and the length is 0.5. If your machine does not have blind hem stitch or you are unable to reduce the stitch width and length sufficiently, use a narrow, fairly open zigzag stitch. Use an open-toe appliqué foot in place of a blind hem foot for better visibility.

Use monofilament thread in the top of the sewing machine and white thread in the bobbin. By reducing the top tension on the machine, the bobbin thread should not show on top. Practise on a scrap of fabric until you are happy with the results.

When attaching the appliqué pieces, the left swing of the needle should just catch the appliqué edge. The straight stitch is just off the appliqué and runs along its edge. Back stitch a few stitches at the beginning and end of the appliqué to secure the threads.

STEMS

Cut green fabrics into 1⅛in wide bias strips. With wrong sides together, stitch ¼in seam along the long edge. Trim away approximately ⅛in from the seam allowance. Insert the rounded end of the bias bar into the tube of fabric and press flat with the raw edges and seam in the centre of the back.

Cut bias strips into thirty-seven pieces approximately 5½in long, two pieces approximately 7in long for the bottom of the wreath and two pieces 8½in long for the top.

For the corner bunches, cut the three stems beneath the bow approximately 5in long. Those above the bow are cut 5½in long with the exception of the middle one which is cut 7½ in long.

Pin the stems in place, tucking the ends under the preceding strip. It may be necessary to trim a little from the various strips. When you are satisfied with the placement of the stems, stitch them in place using the blind hem stitch appliqué method.

CALYX

Trace around the calyx template onto the dull side of the freezer paper. Sixty-five are required and while each calyx can be cut individually, there is an easier method. Trace several, then stack additional pieces of freezer paper under the tracing, cutting a number of layers at one time. Staple or pin the layers together to prevent them from shifting.

Using a dry iron, lightly press the freezer paper calyx onto the right side of the green fabric. (The shiny side of the paper will stick to the fabric.) Cut out individual calyxes adding ¼in seam allowance on each one.

Peel the freezer paper from the right side of the fabric and place it on the wrong side of the calyx with the shiny side of the freezer paper facing up. Make sure the freezer paper calyx is centred onto the fabric calyx. Roll the seam allowance over and using the tip of the iron, gather the seam allowance around the sides of the calyx as you press. Nick the upper curve seam allowance and iron it down. A seam ripper or tailor's awl is useful to hold tiny gathers as you press. (It also prevents burnt fingers.)

Cut most of the 'tail' off and tuck the little extra under when appliquéing the calyx in place. Pin the calyx in place and appliqué the sides using the blind hem stitch method.

NOTE: Don't stitch the upper curve at this stage. Leave the freezer paper in place until the rosebuds are ready to be inserted.

After the buds are made and are ready to be stitched in place under the top curve of the calyx, remove the freezer paper carefully. Using your fingernail and/or tweezers, loosen the freezer paper, holding the edge of the appliqué to prevent excess pulling on the seams. Make sure the top of the calyx is turned under smoothly after removing the freezer paper. To prevent fraying, remove the paper in each calyx as you are ready to sew each bud in place.

FOLDED BUDS

Fold a 4in square of pink fabric diagonally with wrong sides together. Fold each side in towards the centre using the step-by-step photographs as a guide. Turn

Fold 4in square in half diagonally. Fold each side towards centre and turn back top fold slightly.

back the top fold just a little. This turn-back gives the bud extra fullness. Gather the lower edge and pull gathering to fit the calyx template (approximately 1½in). The gathering is done by hand rather than machine. It is then easier to pull up because of the thicknesses.

Lay the quilt out and arrange the buds in place until you are satisfied with the arrangement of the colours. After removing the freezer paper from the calyx, slip the bud under the upper edge of the calyx and with the help of a seam ripper or tailor's awl, ensure any gathers are lying smoothly under the calyx.

Blind hem stitch in place, sewing approximately ¼in of the rosebud to the backing fabric as well as across the top of the calyx to secure the bud.

LEAVES

Trace the leaves onto the dull side of the freezer paper and make them the same

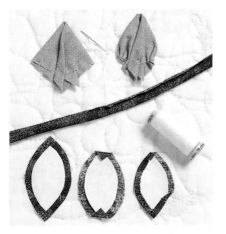

Gather lower edge and pull gathering to fit calyx. For the leaves, press freezer paper shape to right side of fabric.

Close-up of flowers.

ing the appliquéd edges so that the leaves are not pulled out of shape. The small slits can then be hand sewn together, using a herringbone stitch.

HEART WREATH
BOWS

Cut a ¾in wide strip of manilla folder or light cardboard to use as a template when ironing the bows.

Cut 1⅜in wide bias strips of both deep burgundy and dusty pink fabrics and join using 45 degree angles. You will need approximately 110in (2.8m) of each colour.

Centre the cardboard template on the wrong side of the bias strip and press the seam allowances over the template. Give them a light spray of starch to ensure crisp edges.

Pin the bows in place, cut away excess fabric where it overlaps and stitch in place. Stitch the inner edges of the loops first then stretch the outer edges so they lie flat. Stitch as before.

Pin the ties lightly in place, then, after stitching one side of the tie, trim away the excess fabric laying underneath before stitching the next edge.

CORNER BOWS

These narrower bows and ties are made in the same manner as the heart wreath bow but the template is ½in wide and the bias strips are 1⅛in wide. Approximately 180in (4.6m) strips of each colour is required. As the curve of the loop is tighter than that of the large bows, it is necessary to gather the inner curve of each loop lightly.

Distribute the gathers evenly and press when stitching is complete. When pinning the long ties, stretch the edge of the bias strip gently on the outer curves.

BOW KNOTS

Using the templates on the Pattern Sheet, cut one large and one small circle

as you did the calyxes. After peeling the freezer paper from the right side of the fabric, centre the freezer leaf onto the wrong side of the fabric leaf. Turn over the seam allowances at the top and bottom of the leaf. Turn over the side seam allowances, gathering them slightly to ease in the fullness. As with the calyxes, the shiny side of the freezer paper will adhere to the seam allowance and hold it in place while appliquéing.

Pin the leaves in place and appliqué them using the blind hem stitch. Leave the freezer paper intact. When the appliqué is complete, turn the quilt top over and carefully slit the backing fabric behind each leaf.

Using tweezers, carefully pull the freezer paper out through this slit, hold-

from thin cardboard. Trace around the circle onto the wrong side of the fabric with a sharp pencil and cut out, adding a generous ¼in seam allowance. Gather close to the edge of the circle and position the template on the wrong side of the fabric. Pull the gathering tightly and secure it. Press, distributing the gathers evenly. Pop the cardboard out and press again.

You will need four small circles for the corner bows and one large one for the wreath bow.

Appliqué the knots in place to complete the quilt top.

QUILTING

Press the top, taking care not to press the buds. Mark the quilting lines on the fabric. Layer the quilt top, batting and backing and baste the three layers together.

Machine-quilt with a 1¼in diamond grid behind the appliqué flowers.

FINISHING

BINDING

Cut five 2¼in wide strips of damask and join them together to make one long strip. Press this in half lengthwise with wrong sides together. With raw edges aligned, attach the binding to the front of the quilt using a ¼in seam allowance, sewing through all thicknesses and mitring the corners.

Trim away the excess batting and backing. Roll the binding to the back and slip stitch securely in place.

Make a label for the back and sign and date your quilt.

50 Hearts
for 50 Years of Marriage

Memories are made of this. Christine Book designed this heart quilt and it was made by her friend Kaye Harrison, daughter of Ken and Joan Walters, as a gift to celebrate their '50 Golden Years of Marriage'.

A quilt using appliquéd hearts could be made to celebrate any special occasion. It is an ideal way to personalise a quilt, using novelty prints relevant to the recipients.

PREPARATION

CUTTING

For this quilt you will need fifty-four 4¾in squares set in nine rows of six squares each.

From neutral background print A, cut twenty-six 4¾in squares. From neutral background print B, cut twenty-four 4¾in squares.

Finger-press the 12in square of Aida embroidery fabric into four quarters and cut into four 6in squares. If you prefer to work with a larger piece of Aida in a hoop, mark the squares with a pencil and cut them apart after completing the stitching.

From the inner border fabric, cut four 1½in strips across the width.

From the outer border fabric, cut four 4in strips across the width. From the same fabric, cut four 2in strips across the width for the outer binding.

CONSTRUCTION

APPLIQUE

This quilt was appliquéd using the cardboard template method. Trace the heart pattern onto template plastic using a permanent marker or pencil. Cut this out accurately, then trace around this template fifty times onto lightweight cardboard. Cut out these hearts and pin them into position on the back of the chosen novelty fabrics. Position the

Baste novelty print fabric to the cardboard template. Remove template and appliqué to block.

template to make a feature of a particular print if required. Cut out the fabric hearts, adding ¼in seam allowance.

Baste the fabric in place.

NOTE: Be sure to clip the concave top section of the heart and gather the curved edges so the fabric covers the template accurately. Press to 'set' the seam allowance.

Remove the basting stitches and cardboard template and pin a heart in the centre of a 4¾in square. Appliqué in position, using matching thread and a small hem stitch. A fine needle is important for accurate appliqué. Press on the wrong side, when finished. Repeat for the other forty-nine blocks.

CROSS STITCH BLOCKS

Personalise the four Aida blocks with a combination of back stitch and cross stitch embroidery. Consider adding details such as the names of couples, anniversary date, reason for celebration. These embroidered details will need to be drawn onto graph paper to ensure correct placement on the block. Refer to the Cross Stitch graphs on page 46.

Kaye also stitched her parents' signatures on two blocks and you may like to use this idea for your own personalised quilt.

FINISHED SIZE

- Finished quilt size is 89cm x 121cm (35in x 47¾in) approximately. Finished block size is 11cm (4¼in).

MATERIALS

- 60cm (²⁄₃yd) each of two contrasting neutral background prints (background A and background B)
- Collection of scraps of novelty fabrics (picture print fabrics)—allow at least 13cm (5in) square of each
- 30cm (⅓yd) square piece of 14-count cream Aida fabric for embroidering names and wedding details on four squares
- Selection of embroidery cottons
- Embellishments – gold charms, lace, beads, badges, emblems, labels, numerical cake decorations, sequins, novelty buttons
- 1.3m (1½yd) backing fabric if using one fabric OR piece together the leftover novelty fabrics to size
- 20cm (¼yd) bright accent (mustard) fabric for inner border
- 75cm (⁷⁄₈yd) outer border and binding fabric
- Thin quilt batting
- Cream cotton for piecing
- Matching thread for quilting and binding
- 10cm (4in) square of template plastic
- Lightweight cardboard
- 50cm (⁵⁄₈yd) homespun for quilt history envelope on back of quilt (optional)
- Sharp pencil
- Fine needle
- Rotary cutter, ruler and mat

NOTE: All fabric should be 100 per cent cotton, 112cm (44in) wide, pre-washed and ironed. ¼in (6mm) seam allowance is used throughout for sewing and is included in the cutting measurements.

STITCHES USED

Hem Stitch, Cross Stitch, Back Stitch

PIECING

To ensure an overall pleasing design, lay out all the heart blocks in a grid, six blocks by nine blocks, including the four Cross Stitch blocks. These will need to be trimmed to the same size as the heart blocks. When placing the blocks, remember to balance light, medium and dark. **NOTE:** Embroidered blocks look better placed towards the centre of the quilt.

Once you are happy with the block placement, machine piece the blocks together in rows of six, using 1/4in seam allowance. Make nine rows. Sew the rows together in pairs, then the pairs together until the quilt top is completed. For successful construction, ensure the rows are pinned well, that points match and seams lock into place.

 **HELPFUL HINT**

Looking for just the right fabric to symbolise a particular activity or event can be a challenge. Look for fat quarters at quilt shops and ask quilting friends to check their fabric stash.

EMBELLISHMENTS

Once the body of the quilt has been pieced together, add any personalised embellishments and any embroidery of your choice. Be sure to stitch these in place securely.

BORDERS

Carefully press the quilt top, lay it on a flat surface and using a rotary cutter, ruler and mat, square up all the edges. Ensure the top and bottom measurements are the same and that both side measurements are equal.

Measure the length and width through the centre of the quilt top. Adjust two of the inner border strips to the length measurement. Pin these strips to the sides, right sides together, then stitch in place. Press carefully so that the seam allowances face away from the centre of the quilt. Adjust two strips to the new width measurement. Pin to the top and bottom and stitch in place. This butt-joins the border strips. Adjust the measurements of the outer border strips, taking into account the inner border. Add the outer border in the same

manner – first the sides, then the top and bottom.

BACKING

The backing for your quilt could be made from one length of fabric that is slightly larger, 3in all the way around the quilt. Alternatively the back of this quilt can be made a feature by making a 'scrap' backing. Gather together all your leftover pieces of novelty fabric and sew them together at random. It's easiest to stitch together five or six smaller pieces to form a larger unit. Do this several times, then join these units together to form one piece larger than the quilt top.

QUILTING

Layer the quilt top, batting and backing fabric. Baste as you prefer. Hand or machine quilt the layers together. This quilt is quilted by hand, in the ditch between all blocks using a thread to match; in the ditch around the border strips, using a thread to match; and in the wide border, using a simple cable design. Trim any excess batting and backing level with the top.

FINISHING

❖

BINDING

Fold and press the four binding strips in half, wrong sides together. Pin a strip of binding to the right side of the top and bottom of the quilt. Sew in place and trim off any excess binding. Fold to the back, pinning it into place. Extra length will need to be added to the side binding strips – use the leftover from the top and bottom. Sew the binding to the sides and fold to the back. Slip stitch in place, neatly folding in the raw edges of the side bindings.

ROD POCKETS

Cut the rod pockets 4in x 32in, fold them in half, right sides together and stitch along the length and one end with ¼in seam. Pull through to the right side. Hand stitch the open end closed. Hand sew the 1¾in pockets in place, ½in from the top and bottom of the quilt leaving both ends open.

QUILT ENVELOPE POCKET

Make a homespun envelope pocket for the back of the quilt using the pattern on page 47. Fold the homespun in half. Transfer the pattern and markings to the wrong side of one half. Fold the homespun, right sides together. Pin in place and stitch around the edges on the marked line. Turn sharply at inside points, leaving an opening to turn through. Trim seam allowances to ⅛in. Clip the corners.

Turn envelope pieces right side out, pushing out the corners. Press. Whip stitch the opening closed. Stitch ⅛in from the edge. Fold the sides, bottom and top along markings. Press in place. Stitch where the bottom and sides meet to hold the envelope in place. Sew a button on the outside flap and a cotton loop to close. Slip stitch the envelope to the back of the quilt so that the stitching does not show through.

Place the cards, 15cm x 21cm containing the history of the quilt inside the envelope.

The pocket on the back of the quilt with background information on each of the cards.

CROSS STITCH GRAPH
FOR CELEBRATION
SQUARE

GRAPH FOR PATTERN
ON SIGNATURE/
NAME SQUARES

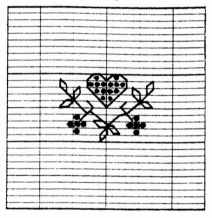

	Light Green
C	Dark Green
●	Apricot
✳	Dark Apricot
✕	Gold

Insert date between lines

CROSS STITCH GRAPH
FOR DATE SQUARE

 110%

OUTER BORDER
QUILTING DESIGN

4 ¼ APPLIQUED HEART BLOCK

HEART
TEMPLATE

PATTERN FOR ENVELOPE
FOR BACK OF QUILT
(Quarter section)

134%

Bridal Wreath Cushion

*Elegant butterflies surround a traditional appliqué design
of hearts and leaves in this delightful cushion.
Cool blues in contrasting shades and patterns give
a variation of the Bridal Wreath block.*

PREPARATION

From the patterns provided, trace each pattern onto template plastic and cut out using scissors.

Place the templates onto thin cardboard and cut out the shapes. You will need eight leaves, four large hearts, four small hearts, four arcs.

Place the cardboard templates onto the wrong side of your chosen fabrics and draw around the shapes with a sharp pencil. Using the quilter's ruler, draw in the seam allowance. This is your cutting line.

CONSTRUCTION

APPLIQUE

Arcs

Baste the outer curve first, then the inner curve, nicking the seam allowance as you go. Do not baste the ends of the arcs under as these will be sewn into the seam allowances.

Leaves

Baste under the point first, turn over seam allowance to just before the next point, turn under the point, then continue around the leaf.

Hearts

Turn under the point, fold over the seam allowance, baste to the centre of the heart, nick the seam allowance, then continue down to the point.

Once all the pieces have been basted, spray the back with spray starch and press with a hot iron.

Cut out a 13in square of background fabric. Remove basting from the shapes, and pull out the cardboard. Refer to the

photograph of the cushion and pattern and place the fabric pieces onto the background square to form the design. The raw edges of the arcs should line up with the raw edges of the block. Make sure the arcs are an equal distance apart on all four sides. Baste them into position. Using threads to match the fabrics, use small hem stitches to stitch the pieces into position.

When finished, cut the background square into a 12½in block, making sure the appliqué is centred in the square.

Borders

From the border fabric, cut two 2in x 12½in strips and two 2in x 15½in strips.

Stitch the two shorter strips to the opposite sides of the square, then add two larger strips to the remaining opposite ends.

QUILTING

Draw a 1¼in grid onto the background square starting from the corners. Repeat in the opposite direction across the top of the cushion.

Cut the batting and backing fabric into a 16in square.

Baste the cushion top, batting and backing together, starting from the centre, basting approximately 3–4in apart. Also baste in the opposite direction. Quilt the three layers together using small, even running stitches. Quilt only the background fabric up to the appliqué shapes. Trim back the batting and backing until they equal the cushion top.

FRILL

To make the frill for the cushion, cut three strips of fabric to form a strip measuring 4½in x 110in. Join the three strips into a circle and press it in halves

FINISHED SIZE

• Finished cushion size is approximately 38cm (15in). Finished Block size is 30cm (12in).

MATERIALS

• Small quantities of three different fabrics for two sets of four hearts and eight leaves

• 1.2m (1⅓yd) fabric for borders, frill, cushion backing and arcs of Bridal Wreath pattern

• 36cm (14in) square fabric for background

• 45cm (½yd) square fabric for back of cushion top

• 45cm (½yd) square of batting

• 25cm (10in) zipper

• 45cm (½yd) cushion insert

• Template plastic

• Quilter's ¼in ruler

• Quilting cotton

• Thin cardboard

• No 9 Betweens quilting needle

• Thread to match fabrics to be appliquéd

• Quilting hoop

• Sharp pencil

• Scissors

NOTE: All measurements are based on 115cm (44in) wide fabric.

STITCHES USED

Hem Stitch, Running Stitch,
Gathering Stitch

Basting the appliqué shapes to the cardboard templates ready to stitch to the background fabric.

with the wrong sides and raw edges together. Sew two rows of gathering right around the raw edge of the frill. Divide the circle into halves and then quarters, putting a pin or a coloured thread at each of these points.

Pull up the gathering thread carefully so the frill fits around the cushion, distributing the gathers evenly between the pins at the half and quarter points. Place the frill onto the cushion, raw edge to raw edge and curve it slightly at the corners. Stitch the frill into position on the cushion.

CUSHION BACK

For the cushion back, cut two 9in x 17in pieces of fabric (slightly larger than needed). Stitch the zipper into position between two fabric pieces to form the back of the cushion. Undo the zipper about 4in.

FINISHING

❖

Place the back of the cushion onto the front, right sides together. Pin them into position and stitch together on the stitching line of the frill, ensuring the frill does not catch in the seam. Turn right sides out to check that the frill is sitting neatly. Turn back, trim the raw edges and zigzag or overlock to neaten the edges. Put in the cushion insert.

 HELPFUL HINT

This block can be made into an attractive quilt. When the blocks are butted together without sashing, a secondary pattern of a circle with hearts in it will emerge.

QUARTER SECTION OF APPLIQUE DESIGN

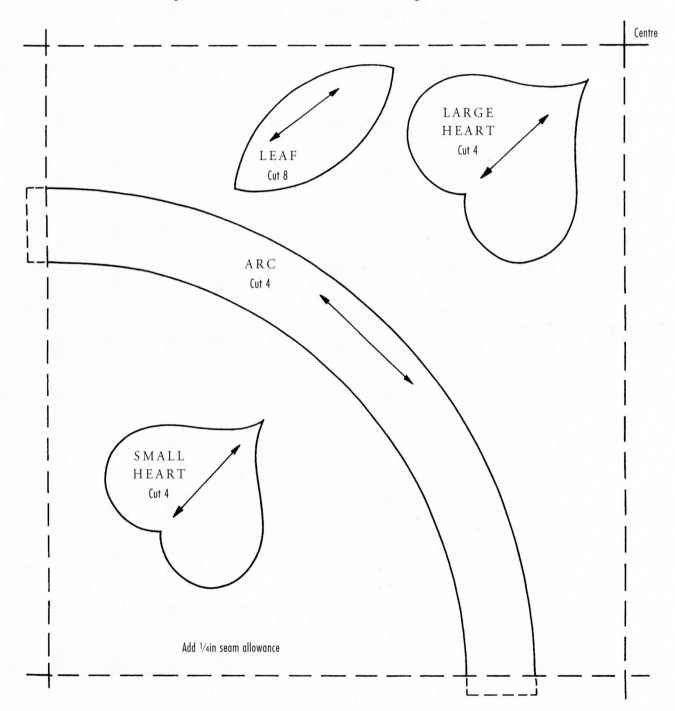

Centre

LEAF
Cut 8

LARGE
HEART
Cut 4

ARC
Cut 4

SMALL
HEART
Cut 4

Add ¼in seam allowance

SS

Bright & Beautiful

*There is such creative pleasure in stitching a quilt with the recipient
in mind and extra delight if that quilt is for a child.
Memories of the joys of childhood are reflected in these special quilts
created for the very young — and the young at heart! Be encouraged by the
imagination, creativity and skill of some of Australia's top quilt makers.*

Simply Bright and Wonderful

This vibrant quilt has fabulous fun motifs to appliqué.
Ideal to make as a first quilt, it uses strips for
the machine-pieced blocks, finished with hand-appliquéd motifs,
contrasting embroidery and hand-quilting.

This quilt is made from twelve randomly pieced rectangular blocks, which are appliquéd, then joined together with sashing strips in four rows of three. The rows are then joined together with horizontal strips.

There is no pre-determined way to make the blocks – you are the artist and can determine which fabric strips you will combine to make up the required size.

For this quilt, the fabric has been torn along the grainline, rather than cutting with scissors or a rotary cutter. However, the instructions have been written with conventional methods to achieve the same results. Each section is prepared on a 'cut as you go' system.

PREPARATION

Wash all fabric scraps in warm soapy water before beginning and iron. If using bright fabric, make sure all colours are safe and will not bleed into your work. As this is a bed quilt, it will become grubby and need to be washed regularly so the fabric must be colourfast.

CONSTRUCTION

THE BLOCKS

This quilt requires a total of twelve blocks each measuring 9½in x 11½in.

For each block, first choose a main colour, smaller than the finished block size, then add a piece of different coloured fabric to either the bottom, side or top. Keep adding strips of fabrics until the piece becomes the required

size. This can be done on the machine or in a small running stitch by hand. Each block should be made of different scraps and no two blocks should be of the same pattern. The fun part in making this type of block is that any piece of fabric will do. Just keep adding scraps until it measures the correct size! Make twelve wonderfully colourful blocks. Decorate with rickrack braid on selected seams now if desired.

APPLIQUE

Trace the shapes onto thick cardboard and cut out to use as templates. Trace around each template onto the front of the appliqué fabric scraps using the quilt photograph as a guide to placement.

Cut out the shapes leaving a small seam allowance around each one. For the appliqué, use a seam allowance of ¼in (6mm) as it is easier to turn under with the needle. Cut into any corners and with a matching thread, needle-turn appliqué each piece onto the main centre fabric of each block. (You can use any method of appliqué to do this.)

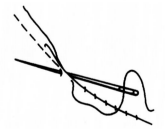

Needle-turn Appliqué

For the sheep and bird designs, back stitch the legs in two strands of the embroidery thread. The little crosses next to the sheep are stitched in six strands. The eyes are cut out of felt so no seam allowance is necessary. When all twelve blocks are complete, press with a hot iron so all the seams are laying flat.

FINISHED SIZE

- Finished quilt size is 135cm x 190cm (53in x 75in). Finished block size is 23cm x 28cm (9in x 11in).

MATERIALS

- Assortment of thirty different fabric scraps to make up the twelve blocks. Each block uses two, three or four contrasting scraps to make up to a size of 25cm x 29cm (9½in x 11½in) including seam allowance

- Small pieces of fabric for appliqué in approximately seventeen different colours

- Eight contrasting scraps of fabric from each of which can be cut a rectangle 9cm x 29cm (3½in x 11½in) for the sashing strips

- Five contrasting fabric strips at least 6cm x 85cm (2½in x 33½in) for the horizontal strips

- 1.5m (1¾yd) fabric for lengthwise borders

- 2.8m (3yd) backing fabric

- 1.4m x 2m (1½yd x 2¼yd) medium-weight batting

- Approx 7m (7¾yd) of 6cm (2½in) wide binding strip made up of leftover scraps

- Assorted embroidery threads

- Small scrap of felt

- 50cm (⅝yd) of two or three different rickrack braids

- No 9 straw needle for appliqué

- No 7 crewel needle for embroidery and quilting

- Thick cardboard

HELPFUL HINT

When selecting fabrics for the appliqué motifs, remember that plain colours on a strongly contrasting plain background will give the image a clearly defined outline. Bright plains on a white background will soften and enhance the colour.

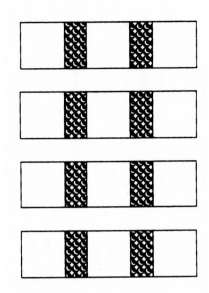

Diagram 1
Sew the blocks together in rows with the sashing strips.

JOINING THE BLOCKS

The blocks are joined together in rows of three with two sashing strips. Cut eight sashing strips, each 3½in x 11½in (see Diagram 1). Make four rows. Press them well. Measure the width of the joined rows.

Cut five horizontal strips from different coloured fabrics, 2½in x the width (approx 33½in). With right sides together, stitch the horizontal strips to the top of each row of blocks.

The fifth strip goes at the bottom of the last row. Join the rows together.

BORDERS

Measure the quilt through the centre, lengthwise and widthwise. Cut two pieces of border fabric 10½in wide x the length of the quilt (approx 54in). Stitch to sides with right sides together. Iron the border pieces open.

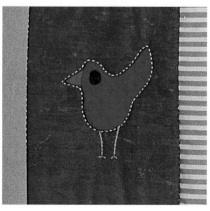

Cut two pieces 10½in x the width of the quilt including the side borders (approx 33in). With right sides together, join these to the top and bottom of the quilt. Press well. The quilt top is now ready to add batting and backing.

BACKING

Cut and join the backing fabric to make a piece 54in x 87in. Check this size to suit your finished top. Lay the backing fabric right side down, then place the batting on top and the finished top piece on the batting with the right side facing up. Baste all three layers together and trim so they are the same size.

QUILTING

Quilt around each block and along each horizontal strip in the ditch. With two strands of different coloured embroidery threads, outline each shape in a decorative running stitch. This is best done approximately ⅛in (3mm) away from the shape so that the stitching can be seen.

The squares have decorative stitching in six strands of thread. Buttons are an optional extra that can be added at this stage, before the binding.

FINISHING

BINDING

Using all the leftover scraps in a variety of colours, make a binding strip 2½in (6cm) wide x approximately 7¾yd (7m) long. Fold the binding in half, wrong sides together and press well. With the raw edges and right sides together, pin and stitch the binding through all three layers, first to the top and bottom, then the two sides. This is best done on a machine and fed carefully so that no puckering occurs. Fold the binding strip over to the back and with a matching thread, slip stitch the binding to the back all the way around the quilt. Tuck the corners under as you go.

All that is left now is to stitch on a label and sign your quilt. Lay it on the bed and enjoy!

106%

106%

Chasing Butterflies

*The 1930s favourite children, Sunbonnet Sue and her companion
Overall Sam, make an enchanting pair on this miniature wall-hanging.
Dainty reproduction prints in yellow, blue and green have been used
for this little quilt picture with fusible hand-appliqué techniques.*

PREPARATION

CUTTING

From the background fabric, cut one strip 3½in x 21in. Cross-cut into six 3½in squares for the blocks.

Cut four lengths, 2½in x 13in for the main border (these are longer than required.)

From each of the six chosen print fabrics, cut for the block borders two lengths measuring 1in x 3½in and two lengths measuring 1in x 4½in.

From the fabric for the binding, cut two strips, 2in wide across the fabric

CONSTRUCTION

APPLIQUE

Trace the required number of shapes from the appliqué patterns onto the paper side of the fusible webbing. Work on only one girl or one boy at a time.

For Sunbonnet Sue, trace the hat, arm and boots in one group and the dress in a second section. Make four.

The Overall Sam pieces can be traced with the hat and boots as one group, the overalls as a second section and the shirt as a third section. Make two.

Cut out the groups of traced shapes for the boy or girl. Do not cut out individual shapes but leave them as a group on the fusible webbing. See the step-by-step photograph below.

Using a medium-to-hot dry iron, press the fusible webbing (paper side up) to the wrong side of the chosen fabric.

The traced shapes can now be cut out exactly on the drawn lines.

Use very sharp scissors and handle fabric carefully to avoid fraying the edges.

Peel the paper backing from the shapes and position them on the background, following the quilt photograph. For Sunbonnet Sue, place the boots first, followed by the dress, hat and arm.

When these are accurately positioned, iron to permanently fuse them to the background. For Overall Sam,

FINISHED SIZE

- Finished quilt size is 31cm x 41cm (12¼in x 16in). Finished block size is 4in.

MATERIALS

- 20cm (¼yd) background fabric
- 15cm (¼yd) fabric for binding
- Small pieces for block borders and appliqué – six prints and three plains, approximately 15cm x 20cm (6in x 8in)
- Stranded embroidery threads to match appliqué fabrics
- Lightweight paper-backed fusible webbing
- 36cm x 46cm (14in x 18in) batting
- 36cm x 46cm (14in x 18in) backing
- No 10 appliqué needle
- Buttons (optional)
- Matching machine embroidery thread
- Sharp scissors

STITCHES USED

Blanket Stitch

Fusible appliqué technique.

Appliquéd centre with block borders ready to sew.

Appliqué patterns for Sunbonnet Sue, Overall Sam and Butterfly.

HELPFUL HINT

By tracing in groups, you will find it easier to keep the small pieces together when pressing the shapes to the fabrics.

place the boots first, followed by the shirt, overalls and hat. Iron to fuse permanently. Blanket stitch around all raw edges using one strand of matching embroidery thread. Start with a tiny knot on the wrong side and bring the needle up on the edge of the shape to be stitched. Keep the stitches tiny and even.

BLOCKS

Following the appliqué instructions, make six little blocks.

Plan your colour scheme as you make these so the block borders will appear in a balanced arrangement. Study the quilt photograph to see how the colours of the block borders have been selected to match the dresses and overalls or shirts of the Sues and Sams.

Sew the 3½in block borders to the opposite sides of the completed blocks. See step-by-step photograph.

Press the seams towards these borders, then sew the 4½in long pre-cut borders to the remaining sides. Press towards this border also.

Alternate the sequence of attaching the block borders to avoid seam bulk. For blocks 1, 4 and 5, join the sides first, then the top and bottom. For blocks 2, 3 and 6, join the top and bottom first, then the sides.

Lay out the little blocks in the planned sequence, following the Quilt Construction Diagram. Sew the blocks together to form three rows of two blocks. Press the joining seams on the first and third rows to the right and press the seam on the second row to the left.

Join these rows together, taking time to match and pin the centre seam before sewing. Press all these seams downward for a neat finish.

BORDERS

Sew the pre-cut border lengths to the sides of the pieced quilt, matching the centres carefully. Press the seams toward this border.

Trim the ends level with the quilt, then sew on the top and bottom borders. Press toward this border and trim the ends level as before.

Trace the butterfly pattern eight times on the paper side of the fusible webbing, leaving some space between each one so they can be roughly cut apart. Make two butterflies from each fabric following the appliqué technique and place them around the border in a pleasing setting. Blanket stitch around each one.

Give the quilt one final press ready for quilting and finishing.

QUILTING

Sandwich the quilt top, batting and backing. Baste the layers together to form a grid of basting over the quilt. Quilt by hand or machine from the centre of the quilt and work outwards in a methodical way. This project is quilted in the ditch between the block borders and around the inside of the blocks. Also quilt around the main section of the quilt before moving on to the border. If you wish, you can sew double wavy lines at regular intervals around the quilt to create a soft basket-weave effect.

Trim the batting and backing back to the quilt top ready for binding.

FINISHING

BINDING

Join the two binding strips together and with wrong sides facing, press in half along the length of the strip. Leaving

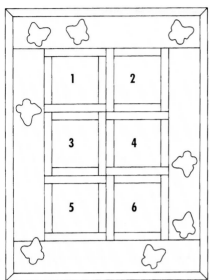

Quilt Construction Diagram

a 2in tail, commence sewing halfway along one side, the raw edges of the binding aligning with the raw edges on the right side of the quilt. Finish sewing ¼in from the end of this side.

Mitre the corner by folding the binding up to make a right angle, then fold the binding down the next side. Make sure that the folded binding is level with the raw edges of the quilt. Continue to sew and mitre each corner.

When you have sewn right around the quilt, back to the starting point, finish sewing approximately 2in from the start of the tail. Remove the quilt

from the machine and take the time to pin and join the ends carefully. To do this, trim the excess binding and insert the end into the beginning which has a seam turned in. Sew this last section together. Turn the binding to the back of the quilt and slip stitch it down by hand. You can sew buttons onto the quilt at this stage if you wish.

It is important to document all the information about your quilt onto a piece of fabric, using a permanent marker pen or a needle and thread. Slip stitch the label to the back of the quilt and sign and date it.

Tu-whit, Tu-whoo
Away with You

Appliqué owl shapes are cut out and applied to the background of this cute quilt, using Vliesofix. The shapes are then machine Satin stitched to make this whimsical little wall-hanging.

PREPARATION

CUTTING

From the light background fabric, cut four pieces; from the dark background fabric cut five pieces and from the iron-on stabiliser cut nine pieces, all 7½in x 10½in.

From the sashing fabric, cut twelve strips 1½in x 7½in and twelve strips 1½in x 10½in.

From the darker blue border fabric, cut two 2in x 30in and two 2in x 38in strips. (These measurements allow for mitred corners.)

From the binding fabric, cut sixteen 1½in squares and enough 1½in binding strips to equal 152in.

CONSTRUCTION

APPLIQUE

Cut out the appliqué shapes and apply them using Vliesofix, a fusible webbing with tracing paper on one side. Use an iron-on stabiliser on the back of the work to give a firm surface, then satin stitch the shapes by machine. Tear the iron-on stabiliser away from the back once the stitching is completed.

Trace out each part of your design separately as shown – owls, beaks, branches, leaves and gumnuts – leaving a small margin of Vliesofix around each shape. Remember that when you trace onto Vliesofix, the design will finish up the reverse image of your tracing, so trace the branches, leaves and flying owl facing the opposite direction to the finished design.

Using medium heat, iron the shapes onto the appropriate fabrics. Cut out the shapes exactly on the cutting line.

Peel off the backing paper from each shape as you arrange each owl on their background panels – four on light fabric and four on dark. The branch should sit 5½in up from the bottom left corner, the owl under the branch and 2in down from the top. On the fifth dark panel arrange a branch, leaves and gumnuts only at this stage.

Using a medium heat, iron the pieces carefully into place making sure they are all firmly attached.

MACHINE EMBROIDERY

Iron a piece of the iron-on stabiliser to the back of each panel again using a medium heat iron. Mark in each owl's features and wings with a pencil using the pattern as a guide.

Using machine embroidery rayon will give a lovely sheen to your work. In the bobbin use Bobbinfil. This is a fine thread which works well with the rayon thread. Dark brown rayon thread is used to outline the owls on the dark backgrounds and a gold metallic thread is used for the owls on the light backgrounds.

When using metallic thread, remember to use a Metafil needle in your machine. This needle has a much bigger eye which allows the thread to pass through easily. Adjust your setting to a fine zigzag stitch. The owls were worked on a stitch width of 2, the branches and leaves slightly less.

Lower the top tension a little. If it is normally 4, lower it to 3. If you do not have numbers on your tension, turn it towards the minus symbol or to the left. Do a test sample of the same fabrics you are using, including a piece of appliquéd fabric with the iron-on stabiliser attached to the back.

When the satin stitch setting is correct, you should be able to see a line of top colour thread on either side of the bobbin thread on the back of your work.

FINISHED SIZE

• Finished quilt size is 71cm x 93cm (28in x 36½in).

MATERIALS

• 30cm (⅓yd) light blue background fabric
• 30cm (⅓yd) dark blue background fabric
• 30cm (⅓yd) pale sashing fabric
• 30cm (⅓yd) darker blue border fabric
• 25cm (10in) brown fabric for corner squares and binding
• 25cm (10in) gold fabric for owls
• Small scraps of dark fabric for beaks
• Scraps of two or three shades of green fabric for leaves and branches
• 1m (1⅛yd) backing fabric
• Sufficient batting
• 50cm (⅝yd) Vliesofix
• 60cm x 101cm (⅔yd x 40in) iron-on stabiliser
• Sixteen 12mm glue-on or stitch-on eyes
• Craft glue
• Twenty-four ⅝in star sequins
• Twenty-four clear seed beads
• Rotary cutter and mat
• Sewing thread for piecing backgrounds
• Rayon machine embroidery threads for appliqué
• Bobbinfil
• Monofilament thread for bobbin when machine quilting
• Polycotton to match backing fabric for bobbin when machine quilting
• Sewing machine with walking and darning feet
• Metafil machine needle
• Pencil
• Scissors for paper and fabric

STITCHES USED

Satin Stitch, Zigzag Stitch

Trace the pattern shapes onto the Vliesofix, then iron them onto the fabric and carefully cut around the shapes.

Layer the various elements of the design on the background fabric and fuse using a medium heat iron.

To start and stop the satin stitch, either work three or four stitches on the spot or pull the threads through to the back and tie them off securely.

Work the satin stitch so that it is mainly on the appliquéd pieces, just coming over slightly onto the background fabric.

When going around curves, 'stop, pivot and turn' the work as necessary to stitch around the curves smoothly. To do this, stop with the needle in the fabric on the outside (widest part of the curve). Lift the pressure foot, turning the work a little, lower the pressure foot, do a few more stitches. The aim is to always have your stitching at 90 degrees to the edge of the appliqué.

Stitch the owl first, stopping and starting on either side of the branch. Stitch the features, wing markings

and beak. Machine stitch the claws with a tapering satin stitch curving slightly outwards or alternatively, hand embroider them in place.

Stitch the gumnuts and leaves, then the branch, joining the leaves and gumnuts to it with the satin stitch or with hand embroidery.

If desired, stitch the vein lines on the leaves with either free machine embroidery or by hand.

Tear away the stabiliser on the eight panels with the owls, but leave it there on the ninth panel.

Join the panels together with the sashing strips and 1½in squares. Refer to the photograph. Add the dark blue border, mitring the corners.

Press all the seams, but do not iron any more than necessary on the stabiliser backing still on the ninth panel.

Place and iron the flying owl into position. You will need to add small pieces of stabiliser to the back where the wings overlap the sashings and border. Satin stitch around this last owl and remove the stabiliser.

QUILTING

Pin or baste the backing, batting and well-pressed quilt top together.

This quilt has been machine quilted using monofilament thread (clear over the light fabric and smoky over the dark fabrics) in the top of the machine and polycotton to match the backing in the bobbin.

When using monofilament thread, begin and end all lines of stitching with six or seven tiny stitches, then increase the stitch length to a little longer than normal sewing stitch. If you normally stitch on 2.5 then increase it to nearly 3.

The quilting is worked mainly in straight lines 'in the ditch' using a walking foot. Do not stitch over the appliquéd shapes. Stitch up to them, finish off with tiny stitches, drag the thread across and begin again on the other side. The threads can be cut off later. Outline the owls, branches, leaves and gumnuts using a darning foot and free machining, or alternatively, quilt them by hand.

FINISHING

Attach the binding around the quilt in your preferred way. Using craft glue, attach the eyes to the owls or sew them on if you are using the stitch-on eyes.

Stitch on the stars using doubled

monofilament thread. Tie a double knot in the end of the thread. Beginning on the front of the work, take three or four small stitches to secure them in place. Thread a star sequin and a seed bead onto the needle and stitch right through the quilt twice, bringing the thread back to the right side and securing it under the star with three or four small stitches.

Make a rod pocket or loops and attach them to the back of the quilt ready for hanging on the wall.

Make a label for the back and sign and date your quilt.

126%

The Three Little Kittens

*Everyone loves the traditional nursery rhyme
about three mischievous kittens and this picture quilt
tells the story in appliqué. It also makes a delightful
wall decoration for a child's bedroom.*

Please read all the instructions carefully before commencing this project.

All measurements include ¼in seam allowances. All the pattern pieces are supplied on pages 78 and 79. Although it will not affect your quilt, it should be noted that when using Vliesofix, appliqué pieces will always be mirror-reversed from the pattern. This can be remedied, if desired, by tracing the pattern from the back with the aid of a lightbox, or taping the patterns to the window when tracing with a pencil onto the Vliesofix.

PREPARATION

CUTTING

Cut the border strips first and work with the remainder for the smaller pieces required for the bed sections.

Border One

Using the mustard fabric, cut two 3in strips across the width of the fabric. Cross-cut into two 20in strips for the horizontal borders and two 17in strips for the vertical borders.

Border Two

Using the striped fabric and working with the length of the stripe, cut two 2½in x 17in strips of fabric for the verticals and two 4in x 29in strips of fabric for the horizontal pieces.

Bed Section

From the green fabric, first cut a 20in x 1¾in horizontal strip for the base of the bed section.

For the lattice section between each bed (A), cut four 2½in x 11½in strips of fabric.

For the section behind the bed heads (B1), cut three 3in x 4½in rectangles.

From the other fabrics, cut the pillows (B2), cut three 2½in x 4½in rectangles from the striped fabric.

For the quilts (B3), cut three 5in x 4½in rectangles from the checked fabric.

For the mats (B4), cut three 2½in x 4½in rectangles from the tan or the mustard fabric.

CONSTRUCTION

Vliesofix Appliqué

Using a pencil, trace the appliqué patterns onto the smooth side of the Vliesofix. Place the pieces to be applied to the same colour (e.g. all gold flower pieces) together. This will ensure you use your Vliesofix and fabric economically.

Using sharp scissors, cut roughly around the traced designs. Do not cut on the lines at this stage.

Press and fuse to the wrong side of the selected fabrics.

Cut accurately along the traced lines and remove the backing paper.

When placing the appliqué pieces, it is a good idea to work on your ironing surface, so that once positioned, the pieces will not have to be moved.

Position on the background, taking care that underlapping and overlapping pieces are positioned accurately, and ensuring that the leaves hide the raw edges of the stems. When the pieces are positioned correctly, fuse them in position with your iron. (Take care that the pieces are in the correct position as once they are ironed, it is almost impossible to shift the pieces without fraying the edges of the fabric.)

Position one stem at a time, then press to fuse the stem prior to the placement of the next one (except when the stems under and overlap) for easier handling.

FINISHED SIZE

- Finished quilt size is approximately 72cm x 60cm (28½in x 23½in).

MATERIALS

For the bed sections you will need:

- A fat quarter or 20cm (¼yd) for the centre green section

- The pillow stripe is included in Border Two requirements

- **Checked Quilts**, 25cm x 40cm (⅓yd x ½yd)

- **Mats**, 13cm x 23cm (5in x 9in) approx (or may be cut from mustard fabric quantities included in Border One requirements)

- **Bed heads and bases**, 25cm (10in) square

- **Kittens**, 20cm (8in) square

- **Border one** (Mustard), 20cm (¼yd)

- **Border two** (Stripe), 30cm (⅓yd) or 75cm (⅞yd) if the stripe runs lengthwise

- **Stems and leaves**, 25cm (10in) square of each of two different greens

- **Dyed fabric for ivy leaves**, 15cm (6in) square

- **Flowers**, three or four different colours, 20cm (8in) square of each

- Matching embroidery thread

- 40cm (½yd) Vliesofix

- 65cm (¾yd) backing

- 65cm (¾yd) batting

- 25cm (⅓yd) binding

- Six or more assorted buttons for flower centres

- Small amount of template plastic for leaf and petal templates

- Quilting thread and scissors

- Acrylic paints, pencils, small amount of wool yarn

- Rotary cutter, mat and ruler, bias bar

STITCHES USED

Buttonhole Stitch, Stem Stitch

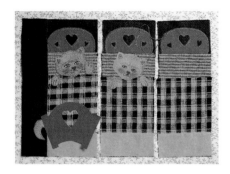

Bed chain-sewn together with one vertical lattice strip attached and tail and bed in position. Kittens' heads and paws are in place and Buttonhole Stitch has started on the centre kitten's face.

Bed Sections

Sew with ¼in seams throughout and press gently after stitching to ensure they lay flat.

Cut out the bed head pieces along the lines. Cut out the hearts, by cutting into the centre with scissors, then inserting small scissors into the slit. Carefully remove the backing paper from the bed head pieces.

Place in position with the bottom of the bed heads at the base of the B1 pieces so the raw edges of both will be within the seam allowance.

Press to adhere. Detail of the bed section construction is shown in the step-by-step photograph.

Place sections B1 and B2 right sides together and stitch using ¼in seams. Chain-sew through all three pairs.

Repeat this technique, when sewing the B3 and B2 sections together and chain-sew through all three.

Repeat, sewing sections B4 to B3 to complete the piecing of the bed sections (see Diagram 2). The bed ends are applied later.

Kitten Faces and Paws

Following the Vliesofix application instructions, trace the designs onto the smooth side of the Vliesofix and iron the Vliesofix onto the back of the kitten fabric.

Ensure that the kittens' face markings are transferred to the back of the Vliesofix, or alternatively put fabric (over pattern) to the light (against a window or over a lightbox) and trace directly onto the fabric with a brown marking pen. Remove the Vliesofix paper from the kittens' faces.

Painting the Faces

Trace over the features with a brown fabric pen. Paint the white eye area. Paint the nose and mouth (or use a fabric pen). Paint the iris in a greenish colour. Highlight one side of the iris with a little yellow. Add the black pupil. Add a white dot (sparkle) to the eye. If desired, outline the outside of the eyes in black.

Shade the cheeks and ears with pink crayon, pencil or blush. Ensure that the pupils and dots are at the same side and height in each eye, otherwise the eyes will look cross-eyed. Mark the claws on the feet with the brown pen.

Positioning Kittens

Place in position, allowing the chins to overlap the quilts. Each kitten's head can be positioned at a different angle to add interest. See the quilt photograph

Apply the Vliesofix to the leaf fabric and cut bias strips with a rotary cutter. Use templates for tracing leaves directly onto the Vliesofix.

Cutting flower petals. Gold fabric has Vliesofix with shapes marked, ready for cutting. Blue fabric shows petals cut and whole flowers partly cut.

Using a bias bar to make the stems. Fold bias strips wrong sides together and sew along length, ensuring bias bar will fit. Insert bias bar, twist seam to back and press.

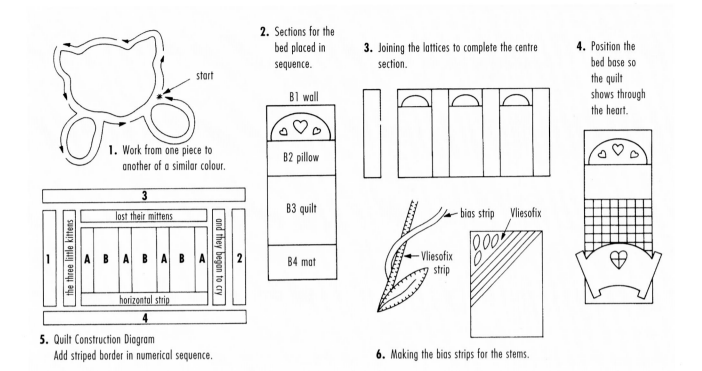

1. Work from one piece to another of a similar colour.

2. Sections for the bed placed in sequence.

3. Joining the lattices to complete the centre section.

4. Position the bed base so the quilt shows through the heart.

5. Quilt Construction Diagram
Add striped border in numerical sequence.

6. Making the bias strips for the stems.

for suggestions. Add the paws, placing them over the pillow/quilt join, or up from the quilt to give a different effect. Fuse in position with the iron.

When the top sections of the three kitten units have been completed, sew the units together with lattices before completing the bed bases.

FINISHING

❖

BED SECTIONS

Sewing the Lattices

With right sides together, sew an A to the left of each B section, chain-sewing the units. Sew the three A/B pieces together. Add an A to the right-hand side to complete this section (see Diagram 3 for further details).

Sew the horizontal strip right across the base of the bed section (see Diagram 4).

Bed Bases

Place the bed bases in position so that only the quilt (not the floor) shows through the heart. Apply a tail to one bed section, placing a bed base over it to give the effect of the tail coming out from the bed. Fuse both at the same time (see Diagram 4).

Mats

You may like to add some detail to the mat, such as reverse buttonhole to give a fringe effect. Alternatively, embroider a design on the mats or outline the quilt at a later stage as shown.

BORDERS

Border One (Mustard)

Take the 3in strips of mustard fabric cut for the borders. The 20in lengths are for the horizontal strips and the 17in strips are for the verticals.

Ensure that each of the horizontal strips is cut to the same length, and that all of the vertical strips are the same as each other. Pin at each end and in the

centre to avoid stretching while sewing. Sew the horizontal strips first, then attach the vertical strips.

Trace the verse onto the strips using a light source such as a window or over a lightbox.

Highlight the wording with the fabric pen. Alternatively, you could do it lightly with a pencil, then again with the marker.

Lettering can be done before or after the leaves and flowers, whichever you prefer. Lettering may be embroidered using stem stitch if you wish.

> ✂ **HELPFUL HINT**
>
> If using a lightbox, you can print the lettering directly with the pen. If working vertically holding the fabric up to a window, it is easier to use a pencil first.

Border Two (Striped)

Using the strips cut for the striped borders, first add the verticals then the horizontals. See the Quilt Construction Diagram for sequence.

FLORAL APPLIQUE

STEMS

Use a combination of methods for added interest and texture. Use a light green for the bias bar strips and the large leaves and a dark green for the buttonholed stems and the small leaves.

HELPFUL HINT

Use a bodkin or darning needle and strands of wool to thread through the stem to give added dimension.

Bias Bar Method

Using a rotary cutter, cut 1in bias strips.

Fold lengthwise, wrong sides facing. If necessary, join some together for a longer stem. Press the seam open (see step-by-step photograph).

Sew along the length with the bias join to the inside. Insert the bias bar.

Twist the seam allowance to the back of the bar. Press.

The seam allowance may now need to be trimmed slightly.

Remove the bias bar. Place the stem in position, then slip stitch to the background. Each time you come to the end of a strip is the ideal place to add a leaf to conceal the raw edges.

Vliesofix Method

Press the Vliesofix strip onto the fabric across the bias. Cut the bias strips with the rotary cutter the width you want the stem, less than ½in. These strips can now be positioned and fused, then buttonholed into position. The shorter ends of this fabric will be used for the leaves (see Diagram 6).

FLOWERS

Trace onto the Vliesofix from the pattern, then appliqué, using buttonhole stitch (see step-by-step photograph). You can trace each petal separately and build up the flower shape, or trace the whole flower in one piece. The gold flowers have stem stitch with a French knot at the end to add extra dimension.

As you complete the buttonhole stitching on the flowers, bring the thread to the centre and sew on a button.

LEAVES

Prepare as for the flowers. You may wish to make a template to trace around on the leftovers of the Vliesofix section. Don't forget to invert the template to get some variation, or draw freehand. Highlight the veins with stem stitch.

MITTENS

Make one pair of mittens by ironing two mitten shapes back to back and buttonholing around the edge. Hang these from a stem using embroidery floss. The other mittens are buttonholed in position to the quilt top. See quilt photograph for positioning.

HELPFUL HINT

To save time, work from one piece to another of a similar colour while you have that thread. When one piece is finished, go under the work and come up at another piece nearby (see Diagram 1).

STITCHING THE APPLIQUE

Buttonhole or Blanket Stitch

Use two strands to give the effect of the contrasting textures, not just the process of appliquéing the pieces together. However, this is an individual choice. Buttonhole around all raw edges using black or matching thread.

BASTING

Press the quilt top and backing. Lay the backing on a table with right side down. Lay batting on top. Smooth out evenly. Place the quilt top, right side up, on top.

Pin with quilters' safety pins, beginning at the centre and working out. Baste, using large stitches, from the centre out.

QUILTING

Outline-quilt most of the appliqué pieces. In some cases, an extra row has been added to echo the shape. The quilted shape on the beds defines the kittens' shape and links the head to the body. A third row is added to the bed sections in green, while most of the other quilting is done in gold.

The leaves are quilted in two different ways. The appliquéd leaves are extended by 'embroidery floss quilting' and quilted around again in quilting thread.

FINISHING

BINDING

Make the binding from straight or bias strips. If using straight strips, join with bias seams, then press open to reduce the bulk at the joins.

To create a very neat finish with the appearance of mitred corners, use the following method:

Cut the binding strips 2¼in wide and join the strips on the bias to make a long strip, approximately 5in longer than the perimeter of the quilt. Press the seams open. Fold the strip in half lengthwise, wrong sides together. Press.

Start about a quarter of the quilt length from a corner, placing the binding on the quilt top, right sides together.

Stitch using a ¼in seam and leaving a 4in tail at the beginning.

Sew to the corner, stopping ¼in from the edge and back stitch.

Raise the needle and presser foot, remove the quilt and clip the threads.

Fold the binding away from the quilt, forming a 45 degree angle fold.

Using the outside edges of the quilt as a fold-line guide, fold the binding back on itself, forming a pleat and aligning the raw edges of the binding with those of the next side of the quilt.

Position the needle a few stitches beyond the ¼in line from the raw edge.

Back stitch to within ¼in from the raw edges, stop and stitch forward to within ¼in of the next corner. Stop and back stitch.

Continue, repeating on each corner

until the binding is attached to all four sides of the quilt. Stop and back stitch about 6in from where you began stitching. Each corner will have a loose pleat formed by folding the binding.

Place the ends of the remaining unattached binding and the 4in tail right sides together. Adjust them to fit.

Join the ends with a diagonal seam and trim the excess fabric.

Stitch this newly-joined section to the quilt to finish attaching the binding.

Turn the binding to the wrong side, fold and slip stitch down.

Make a label for the back and sign and date your quilt.

TAIL

LEAVES

KITTEN

118%

FLOWERS

LETTERING FOR VERSE

The three little kittens lost their mittens, and they began to cry.

127% then 200%

BED BASE

BED HEAD

118%

It's Wash Day

*Use assorted country scraps along
with mini clothes pegs and buttons to create the
illusion of a new visual dimension.
The naive mini quilts almost seem to blow in the breeze!*

PREPARATION

CUTTING

From the background fabric, cut a rectangle measuring 44in x 19in. From the border fabric, cut three strips 1¼in by the fabric width.

From the country fabric scraps, cut thirty-eight 4½in squares for the block sashing border.

CONSTRUCTION

PIECING

A ¼in seam allowance is used throughout.

Attach a border strip to the top and bottom of the background piece and press. Cut the remaining border strip in half and attach to either end of the background piece. Press and trim.

Make the block sashing border by joining the thirty-eight squares into two rows of twelve and two rows of seven.

Attach the twelve-square units to the top and bottom, press and add the seven-square units to the sides, taking care to match the corner squares of the top and bottom borders. Adjust the seams if necessary. Press.

Layer the backing fabric, batting and background panel. The backing and batting should be about 2in bigger than the pieced top on all sides. Baste the three layers together, paying special attention to the edges.

NOTE: Basting is a big zigzag not a straight baste. This cuts down on the movement between the layers and is an extremely secure stitch.

BINDING

Cut four 4in strips from the binding fabric. Cut 10in off the length of two of the strips and attach to the two remaining strips. These longer strips are for the top and bottom of the quilt and the shorter ones are for the sides. Press all four strips in half lengthwise, with wrong sides together, ready for attaching.

Machine stitch the binding to the top and bottom of the quilt, pin well as this will keep the layers true. Turn back and attach the side bindings in the same manner. Trim off the excess batting and backing fabric. The hanging tabs should be stitched in place at this time. (See instructions for the tabs further on.) Fold the binding to the back and firmly slip stitch in place. Leave the basting in place.

QUILTING

The quilting on the background should be completed before the mini quilts, flowers, trees or clothes line are attached.

Using a lead pencil or water-soluble pen, mark a 2in diagonal grid over the plain centre panel of the quilt and quilt through all thicknesses.

Remove the basting and water-soluble pen marks.

TABS

For the seven tabs, cut seven pieces of fabric 8in x 5½in and seven pieces of Pellon 8in x 3in.

Fold each of the fabric strips in half, then lay a strip of Pellon on top and machine stitch a ¼in seam through all thicknesses on both long sides and on one short side. Trim seams and turn through. Press each piece and slip stitch it invisibly in place at even intervals to the back of the quilt, so the raw edges will be hidden under the turned binding. The spacing between each tab will be about 6in. The first and last tabs should align with the binding.

FINISHED SIZE

- Finished size is approximately 138cm x 75cm (54in x 29½in).

MATERIALS

MAIN QUILT

- 60cm (⅝yd) background fabric
- Approximately twenty-five assorted country scraps large enough to cut several 4½in squares for the block sashing border
- 15cm (¼yd) for first border
- 1.5m (1¾yd) Pellon
- 1.5m (1¾yd) backing
- 70cm (¾yd) binding and tabs
- Heavy jute string
- Quilting cottons
- 8 mini clothes pegs
- 1m (1⅛yd) Vliesofix
- 30cm (⅓yd) of tea-dyed cotton or wool batting
- Black linen thread
- Crochet cotton (20) natural
- Buttons – there is a huge assortment of buttons, ie knots on the tree trunks, on the leaves and butterflies, eyes on the birds and on the mini quilt. Use the quilt picture as a guide and keep your eyes open for interesting buttons
- Velcro spots

NOTE: For the trees, quilts, birds, sunflowers and other appliquéd pieces use the remains of your country scraps and add any additional colours not used in the border.

(materials continued on page 82)

STITCHES USED

Slip Stitch, Running Stitch

Buttonhole Stitch

MATERIALS

MINI QUILTS

- Selected scraps for the appliqué shapes
- Brown and natural-coloured quilting cotton

SUNFLOWER QUILT

- 30cm (12in) square of background fabric
- 30cm (12in) square of backing fabric
- 30cm (12in) square of Pellon
- 10cm x 115cm (4in x 45in) strip of binding fabric
- Hedgehog button

NOAH'S ARK QUILT

- 30cm (12in) square of background fabric
- 30cm (12in) square of backing fabric
- 30cm (12in) square of Pellon
- 10cm x 115cm (4in x 45in) strip of binding fabric
- 4 coconut star buttons
- 1 pair zebra buttons
- 1 pair giraffe buttons

HEART AND FOUR-PATCH QUILT

- Assorted scraps for background
- 30cm (12in) square of backing fabric
- 30cm (12in) square of Pellon
- 9cm x 115cm (3½in x 45in) strip of binding fabric
- 5 small wooden buttons

APPLE PATCH QUILT

- Four, 12cm (5in) squares for the background
- 30cm (12in) square of backing fabric
- 30cm (12in) square of Pellon
- 8cm x 115cm (3¼in x 45in) strip of binding fabric
- 1 heart-shaped button

TREES

NOTE: Remember to position the washing line so that it weaves behind the trees and has a knot in both ends and a dip in the middle.

Using the tree pattern, cut out two tree shapes in Pellon. Trace the tree pattern onto the selected fabric twice (once in reverse), but leave the fabric in a rough rectangle with 1in extra all the way around the tree pattern. Baste the Pellon shapes to the wrong side of the fabric and quilt at random up and down the length of the trunk through both thicknesses. Trim the fabric to ½in from the Pellon, turn under and baste in place.

Position and pin to the quilt (see colour picture) and appliqué into position. Leave an opening on both sides of both trunks for the washing line to be threaded through. Sew several buttons onto the trunk, stitching through all layers, to give the illusion of tree knots. When completed, remove the basting.

Use the same method for the clothes prop, following the pattern provided.

FLOWERS, LEAVES AND BIRDS

The flowers, birds, leaves, sunflowers and stems are made with a Vliesofix and fabric sandwich, backed with tea-dyed cotton or wool batting.

Cut a rectangle piece of fabric, fold in half, press the wrong sides together and open up. Cut a piece of Vliesofix half the size of the rectangle and iron onto the wrong side of one half of the rectangle, peel off the backing, fold the fabric over the Vliesofix and iron. Repeat for several green, yellow, orange, black and grey fabrics. You can make up more sandwiches as required.

Make plastic or paper templates for the flowers, leaves, stems and birds from the designs provided and use these templates to cut the design pieces from the sandwiched fabrics. Use the colour picture as a guide for number and placement. Cut out rough shapes of tea-dyed batting to place under the sandwich shapes and using the linen thread, work a small running stitch around the edge of the shape through all layers. Trim the batting back to the edge. Sew a line of running stitch along the middle of the heart-shaped leaves and gather slightly to give the leaves some shape. Place the flower petals under the centre and catch in place with an additional running stitch. Repeat this method for the birds but use a contrasting natural crochet cotton for the running stitch.

APPLIQUE

For the birds, use a straight stitch to appliqué around the edge, then sew a button through all layers for the eye (see Diagram 1 on page 83).

Attach the heart-shaped leaves with a button sewn through all layers. To attach the base flowers, sew a running stitch as close to the edge of the centre circle as possible, using a dark brown quilting cotton and stitching through all layers of fabric twice.

Attach the sunflower leaves using a straight stitch to appliqué around the edges, as for the bird, and sew them with dark brown thread through all of the layers. Quilt the flower stems using the dark brown cotton and a running stitch sewn through all layers of the fabric. Use the same method for sewing the sunflower heads as used for the base flowers, sewing a running stitch as close to the edge of the centre circle as possible. Leave the petals free to provide a three-dimensional effect.

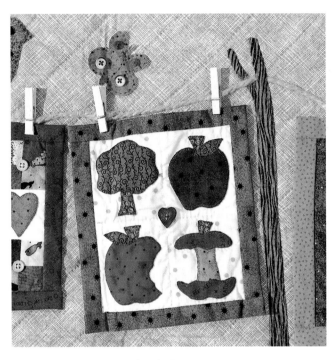

The apple mini quilt pegged to the line.

The appliquéd tree and sunflower with the Viesofix and fabric sandwich flower petals.

MINI QUILTS

SUNFLOWER QUILT

Trace the individual pattern pieces, including overlaps, onto Vliesofix.

Iron the traced shapes onto the chosen fabrics, cut them out and iron into place on the background fabric. Buttonhole stitch around all edges of the plant and pot.

To finish, iron the completed front panel, then layer the backing, Pellon and quilt top and baste them together. Quilt around the edge of each shape using natural cotton. Bind as for the background quilt and add the buttons.

APPLE QUILT

Cut the background panels following the given diagram, but adding ¼in seam allowance to the four sections. Stitch the four sections together. Trace the reversed apple quilt design provided onto Vliesofix, cut out and iron onto

the chosen fabrics. Iron the shapes in place on the pieced background panel. Buttonhole stitch around the designs, then finish in the same manner as the mini sunflower quilt.

Add a heart-shaped button in the centre, stitching through all thicknesses.

NOAH'S ARK QUILT

Following the design diagram provided, cut out the background block adding ¼in seam allowance. Trace the ark and other design components onto Vliesofix, reversing the bird. Cut out the shapes and lay them onto the background. Double check, then iron in place.

Buttonhole stitch around the pieces and finish as for the other mini quilts. Add the star and animal buttons.

FOUR-PATCH AND APPLIQUE HEART QUILT

Cut four 2½in squares for the heart blocks and twenty 1½in squares for the Four-patch blocks.

Diagram 1
For straight stitch appliqué, the small stitches should sit at right angles to the design.

Make the Four-patch blocks first, join the blocks in rows following the diagram provided, then join the rows. Trace the hearts onto Vliesofix and iron them onto the chosen heart fabric. Iron the hearts in place on the plain blocks and buttonhole stitch around each of the hearts.

Finish the mini quilt following the given instructions for the previous quilts, then attach the buttons to the intersection of the Four-patch squares, sewing through all layers.

FINISHING

❖

Thread the jute under the trees and clothes prop and tie a double knot at both ends. Place the pegs on the line and randomly couch stitch the line to the background quilt, making sure the stitch cannot be seen.

Attach the top and bottom of the quilts with ties (crochet cotton) or self-adhesive Velcro spots. Don't tie too tightly, give the quilts some fullness so they appear to be blowing in the breeze as they hang on the line.

Make a label for the back and sign and date your quilt.

APPLE MINI QUILT

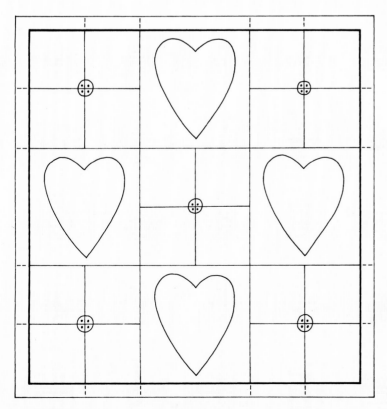

SUNFLOWER MINI QUILT

FOUR-PATCH
AND APPLIQUE HEART
MINI QUILT

166%

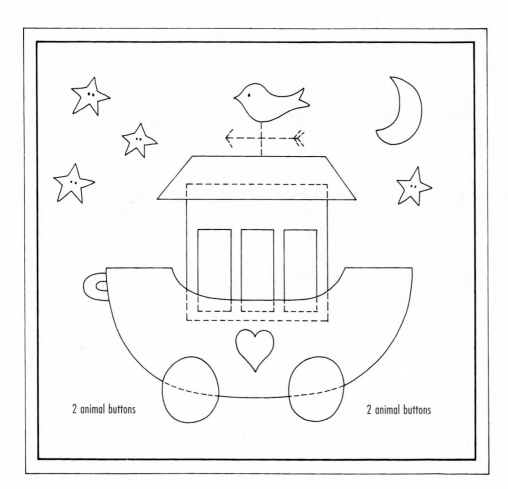

NOAH'S ARK
MINI QUILT

2 animal buttons

2 animal buttons

 166%

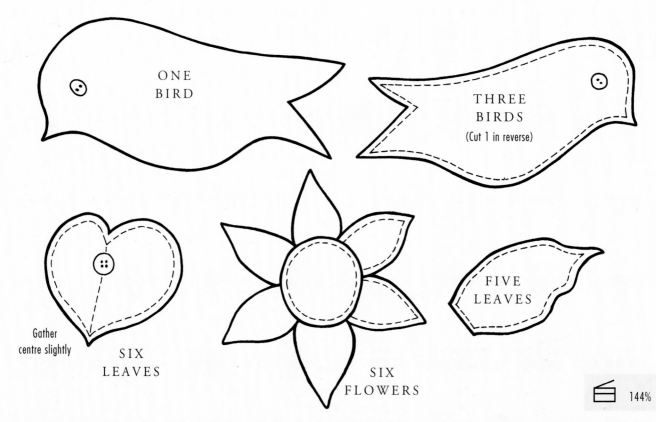

ONE
BIRD

THREE
BIRDS
(Cut 1 in reverse)

Gather
centre slightly

SIX
LEAVES

FIVE
LEAVES

SIX
FLOWERS

144%

FIVE LEAVES

ONE
FLOWER
HEAD

THREE
FLOWER
HEADS

2 BUTTERFLIES

144%

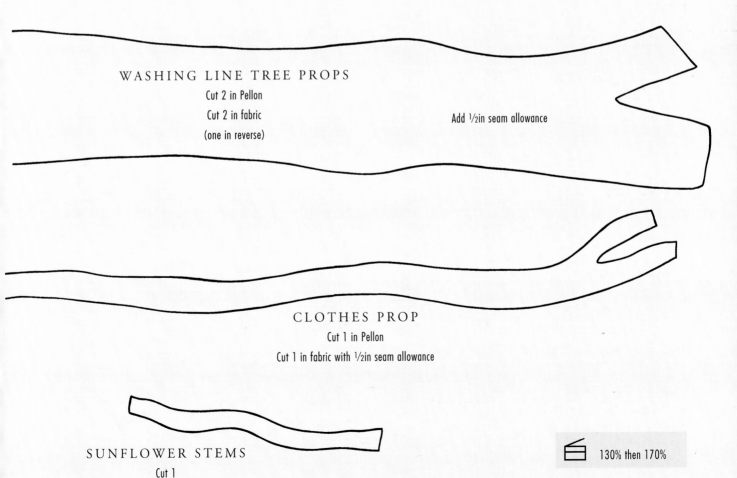

WASHING LINE TREE PROPS

Cut 2 in Pellon

Cut 2 in fabric

(one in reverse)

Add ½in seam allowance

CLOTHES PROP

Cut 1 in Pellon

Cut 1 in fabric with ½in seam allowance

SUNFLOWER STEMS

Cut 1

130% then 170%

Sunbonnet and Flowers

*Sunbonnet Sue takes on a country look
in this cheery little wall-hanging
made in a variety of country coloured fabrics.
Three tiny butterflies add a whimsical touch.*

PREPARATION

All appliqué pieces are attached using the basted method.

Trace all the pattern pieces onto template plastic and cut out carefully.

Using an HB or white pencil, draw around the template onto the right side of the fabric. Cut out each of the individual shapes, leaving a lean ¼in seam allowance.

Using the pencil line as a guide, turn the seam allowance under and baste. You will need to snip almost to the line on the inverted point of the heart and halfway to the line on the concave curves of the watering can spout and the bonnet to enable you to turn these seams under.

Pin the prepared pattern piece into position and sew it to the background using a matching thread and a blind hem stitch. Sew extra stitches in the inverted point of the heart.

Remove the basting stitches then press on the wrong side.

and bonnet from the assorted fabrics.

Cut three tiny butterflies from pre-printed fabric leaving a lean ¼in seam (or use three ceramic buttons if you prefer).

WATERING CANS

For the background, cut one 5¾in x 20¼in block. For each watering can, cut one main piece, one spout and one ¾in x 8in length of bias for the two handles. **NOTE:** Reverse the templates for one of the watering cans.

SASHING AND INNER BORDER

Cut four 1½in wide strips. From these four strips, cut two 12¼in lengths, two 20¼in lengths, two 22¼in lengths and two 23in lengths.

BORDER

Cut one 3in strip of each of the five fabrics. From these strips cut several random lengths such as 3¼in, 5in, 6½in continuing through to the end.

Binding

Cut three 2½in strips of fabric.

CUTTING

HEARTS

For the background, cut one 4½in x 20¼in block. Cut five hearts from assorted fabrics.

SUNFLOWERS

For the background, cut two 6in x 12¼in blocks. Cut two pots and two pot rims, two leaves, twenty petals, two centres and two 1in x 6in lengths of bias.

SUNBONNET SUE

For the background, cut one 7¼in x 12¼in block. Using the templates, cut out the dress, apron, sleeve, hand, shoes

CONSTRUCTION

NOTE: The sewing thread should match the fabric being appliquéd, not the background fabric.

HEARTS

Position and appliqué the basted hearts in a pleasing arrangement of colour on the background fabric.

After completing the appliqué, work a row of blanket stitch around each heart in two strands of embroidery thread.

SUNFLOWERS

Lightly trace the pattern onto the background. (Remember to reverse the second block.)

Draw around templates and cut out with a lean ¼in seam, then using the pencil line as a guide, baste the seam allowance under.

Appliqué the pieces.

BIAS STEM

Press the bias strip in half (with the right side out). Place the raw edges of the bias on the inside curve of the stem line and pin in place. Trim the ends of the bias leaving ½in to go under where the sunflower and the flower pot will be positioned.

Sew this into position using a little running stitch one-third of the way in from the raw edges. Roll the bias stem over the stitching line to cover the raw edges. Pin this in place and appliqué it down using a blind hem stitch.

Place the flower pot and rim on the background and appliqué. Place and appliqué the leaf in position.

Position five petals in a circle so that the edges are just touching. Appliqué

into position. Arrange the next five petals on top of and in between the bottom layer of petals. Appliqué into position as before.

FLOWER CENTRE

Make a cardboard template of the circle. Mark around the template on the wrong side of the fabric and cut out leaving a generous ¼in seam allowance. Sew a little running stitch halfway between the drawn line and the raw edge. Place the cardboard template on the wrong side and gather the thread around the cardboard. Tie the ends of the threads. Press this circle, then ease the cardboard out to use again. The centres can now be appliquéd onto the flowers.

Make two sunflower blocks.

SUNBONNET SUE

Carefully trace the pattern onto the background. Position the prepared pieces on the background commencing with the shoes, followed by the dress, apron, hand, arm and bonnet (in that order). Appliqué into place.

Butterflies can be appliquéd onto the background if desired. (If buttons are preferred, do not sew them on until after the quilting is complete.)

Optional: Using two strands of the embroidery thread, blanket stitch around the sections of Sunbonnet Sue as shown.

WATERING CANS

Carefully position and trace three watering cans on the background block. (Remember to reverse one.) Sew each

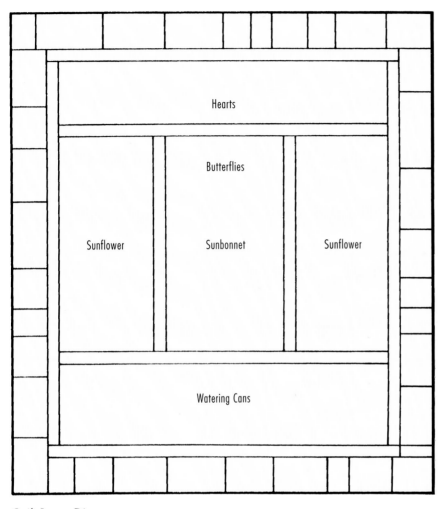

Quilt Layout Diagram

borders. Sew the pieces together for the top and bottom borders. Make each border section longer than required.

Sew the side borders to the quilt and trim the excess length. Add the top and bottom borders and trim as required.

QUILTING

Sandwich the quilt top, batting and backing. Pin or baste the layers, depending on your preferred method of quilting.

The quilt has been machine quilted in the ditch around each block and hand quilted around the appliqué shapes. When the quilting is complete, trim the backing and batting.

FINISHING

BINDING

Sew the pre-cut strips together to form a continuous strip. With wrong sides facing, iron in half along the length. Leaving a 3in tail, sew the binding to the quilt. Matching the raw edges of the binding to the raw edges (on the right side) of the quilt, sew using a generous ¼in seam. Stop sewing ¼in from the end of this side, back stitch and remove the quilt from the machine. Mitre the corner by folding the binding up to make a right angle, then down the next side. The folded binding should be level with the raw edges of the quilt. Continue to sew and mitre each corner. When the starting point is reached, trim the binding and insert it into the tail. Pin carefully before sewing this final section. Turn the binding to the back of the quilt and slip stitch by hand.

Label and date your quilt.

watering can in the following order: side handle, top handle, spout and main section.

The two handles are made using the pre-cut bias strip following the method described for the stem in the Sunflower block. Due to the very tight curves, take care to ease the bias around the curve.

Optional: Using two strands of the black embroidery thread, blanket stitch around the spout and main section of the watering can.

PIECING

Lay out the completed blocks with the pre-cut sashing strips between. See the Quilt Layout Diagram provided.

Join a sunflower block, Sunbonnet Sue and the second sunflower block together with the sashing strips between. Press all seams toward the sashing.

Sew a sashing strip to the top and bottom of this unit. The hearts block can then be added to the top and the watering cans can be sewn to the bottom.

INNER BORDER

Add the inner borders by sewing the pre-cut strips to the sides, then to the top and bottom. Press all seams towards this border.

MAIN BORDER

Place the randomly cut fabrics around the quilt in a pleasing combination. Sew pieces together to create two side

SUE

HEART

WATERING CAN

SS

SUNFLOWER

FLOWER POT

SS

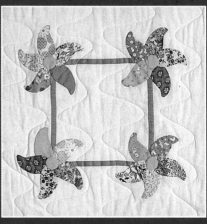

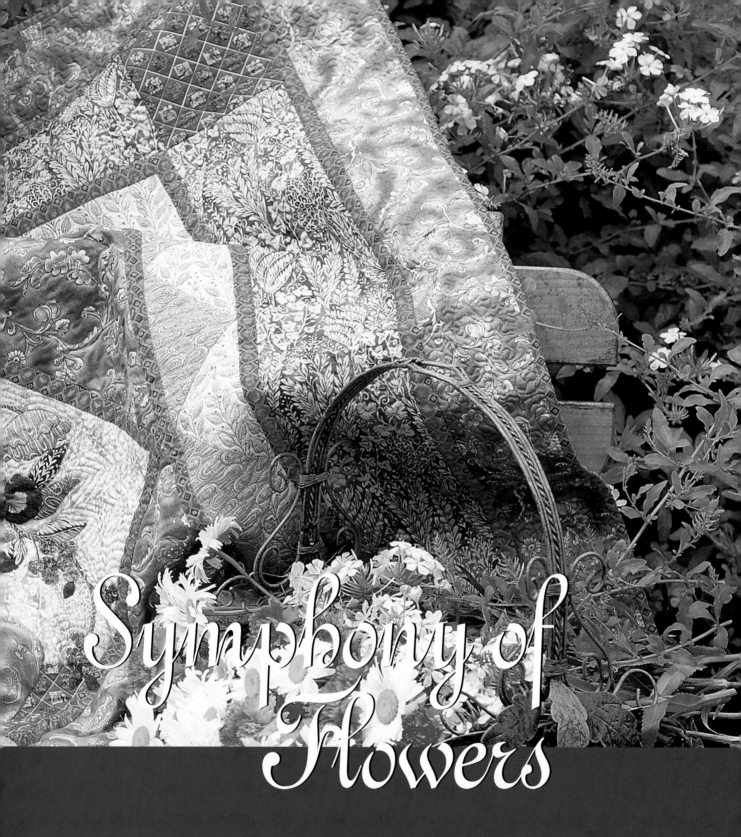

Symphony of Flowers

Sentiments have always been expressed through flowers. This theme has overflowed into appliqué. Circles are gathered into yoyos, with embroidered centres. Roses emerge from layers of gathers. Buds are made from fabric strips or ribbon, with bell flowers tightly gathered at the stem. Create your own special sanctuary with these floral symphonies.

Tall Poppies

The traditional medallion motif of flowers in a vase takes on an Art Deco look in this modernistic appliquéd wall-hanging. Vivid red and yellow poppies are set against a bold black, spotted vase and neutral background fabrics, with the colours reflected in the dramatic sawtooth border.

PREPARATION

CUTTING

Cut one background square for the appliqué, 20½in (52cm).

Cut the top and bottom border from the stripe border fabric, 20½in x 7½in (52cm x 19cm).

Cut two side borders from the stripe fabric 34½in x 7½in (87.5cm x 19cm).

For the binding, cut 2½in (6cm) strips across the width of the red fabric to make 4yd (3.7m).

CONSTRUCTION

This quilt uses traditional appliqué techniques. The appliqué design and templates are given on the Pattern Sheet.

Matching the centre point of the background fabric to the centre point on the pattern, lightly trace the pattern onto the background fabric. Prepare the appliqué pieces as follows:

Trace all the templates from the Pattern Sheet onto lightweight cardboard, marking the appropriate numbers on each shape. For example, you will need one vase and nineteen flower centres. Each number on the design represents the order of stitching, from No 1 through to No 28.

Lay each cardboard pattern piece onto the relevant fabric and trace onto the wrong side of the fabric. Add ¼in (6mm) seam allowance and cut out each shape. Baste the wrong side of each fabric piece to the cardboard templates with a few large basting stitches across the centre of each pattern. Press the seam allowance over the cardboard shape and baste into position.

Using the point of the iron, press all around the piece towards the centre of the card. Remove basting stitches and card, then baste the piece into position on the background.

STEMS

Cut seven bias strips, 1½in (4cm) wide, diagonally across the stem and leaf green print fabric.

Fold the strip in half lengthwise, wrong sides together and machine stitch ¼in (6mm) from the raw edges, making a tube. Slip the Celtic Press Bar into the tube and position the seam at the centre back.

Press the tube flat, with the seam allowance at the back. If necessary, trim the seam so it does not extend beyond the folded edge of the bias.

Remove the bar and baste the stems along both edges into position on the background square.

APPLIQUE

Start with the vase, pattern piece No 1. Using a fine appliqué stitch, sew the sides and base into position, leaving the top of the vase open to allow the ends of the stems to be slipped underneath and 'into' the vase. Appliqué the stems into position. Following the numbering sequence on the pattern pieces, appliqué the remainder of flowers, centres and leaves into position as shown.

When pressing the completed appliqué, lay your work right side down on a towel and gently press the work from the back.

BORDER

Using the triangles for the sawtooth border, start at the centre point of the border section and lay out eight triangles along each section (see Border Layout Diagram). On the side

FINISHED SIZE

• Finished quilt size is 86.5cm (34in) square.

MATERIALS

• 70cm (¾yd) background fabric
• 25½cm (10in) square black fabric for vase
• 1m (1⅛yd) striped border fabric
• 60cm (⅝yd) green print for stems and leaves
• 1m (1⅛yd) red print for flowers, sawtooth border and binding
• 20cm (¼yd) yellow print for flower centres
• 1m (1⅛yd) fabric for backing
• 1m (40in) square of batting
• Appliqué, embroidery and quilting needles
• Lightweight cardboard
• Quilting thread
• Threads to match flowers, stems and vase
• Soft (3B) sharpened pencil
• Celtic Press Bars
• General sewing supplies

It is recommended that fabrics be 100 per cent cotton, 115cm (45in) wide, pre-washed and ironed.

STITCHES USED

Appliqué Stitch

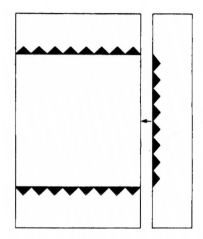

Diagram 1.
*Layout Diagram for Appliqué Sawtooth
Border. Attach top and bottom borders. Add
side border.*

Diagram 2.
*Quilt Layout Diagram. Appliqué outer edges of sawtooth border.
Note the placement of four corner triangles.*

border sections, you will need to mark the finishing point for the triangles, approximately 10¼in (26cm) from the centre of the side border. Appliqué into position, stitching only the two short sides of the triangles as the long side will be included in the seam.

Using a ¼in (6mm) seam allowance, sew the top and bottom border sections to the centre panel.

Add the side borders, taking care to match the sawtooth borders at the corners. Using twelve triangles for each outer edge of the border, start at the centre and appliqué the sawtooth border into position, adding one corner triangle to complete each corner (see the Quilt Layout Diagram).

Appliqué additional stems in a flow-

ing design onto each border. Add the flowers, centres and leaves.

QUILTING

Prepare the quilt top for basting by laying out the backing fabric wrong side up, place the batting on top, then the quilt top, right side up.

Baste with a grid at about every 3in to 4in (7.5cm to 10cm) and trim the backing and batting to fit.

Quilt as desired. A diamond pattern is hand quilted in the background block and the flowers and the yellow centres are highlighted with outline quilting.

FINISHING

❖

Make a label for the back and sign and date your quilt.

BINDING

Using the 2½in (6cm) strips cut from the red print, press the binding in half, wrong sides together. With raw edges together, sew to the quilt top, mitring corners. Attach a sleeve to hang the quilt if desired.

 HELPFUL HINT

When hand quilting, run your thread lightly across a piece of beeswax to prevent it from tangling.

A Quilter's Window Box

*Plaids and checks are delightfully transformed into a
floral vista in this colourful wall-hanging.
The window-frame border emphasises the textures and
raised dimension of the ruched and padded flowers.*

PREPARATION

Using the template plastic, trace all of the flower shapes, petals and the leaves from the templates provided, then cut them out carefully.

For the yoyo flowers and the daisies, using an HB pencil or white pencil, draw around the template onto the wrong side of the fabric. Cut out the individual shapes, leaving a scant ¼in seam allowance.

For the leaves, draw around the template plastic onto the Vliesofix. You will need fourteen light green leaves and nine dark green leaves, varying the shapes between the two fabrics. Cut out the Vliesofix shapes and press them onto the green fabrics, remembering to iron with the glue side down.

Cut the required number of shapes out of the fabric.

CONSTRUCTION

YOYO FLOWERS

Using Template 1, trace nine circles, varying the fabrics. Add ¼in seam allowance before cutting out.

With a stitch length of 4–5, sew inside the ¼in seam allowance, leaving the threads long enough to tie off. Pull the threads together as tightly as possible. Tie them off to secure.

With three of the yoyos, divide each one into five sections. Overstitch the edge at each point, then pull tight and secure.

DAISIES

For the large daisies, choose three fabrics. Using Template 2, trace and cut ten out of each fabric for the outside petals.

Place two petals right sides together and stitch around the outer edge leaving the bottom open. Turn right side out and then press.

Sew across the base of five petals using a long stitch. Gather slightly, pull together and secure.

For the small inner petals, use Template 4 and a contrasting colour. Trace and cut out. Follow the folding instructions as shown in Diagram 1. Stitch to secure.

Place the inner petals on top of and in between the larger petals. Slip stitch them in place.

For the small daisy, use Template 3. Choose one of the fabrics, trace and cut out ten petals.

Template 5 is used to make a yoyo for the centre of the large daisy. Stitch ⅛in from the edge, using a long stitch, leaving the threads long. Place Template 7 inside the circle and gather the threads. Put a little piece of batting between the fabrics and plastic, to add body to the centre. For the small daisy, repeat this technique using Template 7 with Template 6 as the inside circle.

Pull tightly together and spray with starch, then press. Carefully remove the plastic template. Secure with a stitch on top of the petals.

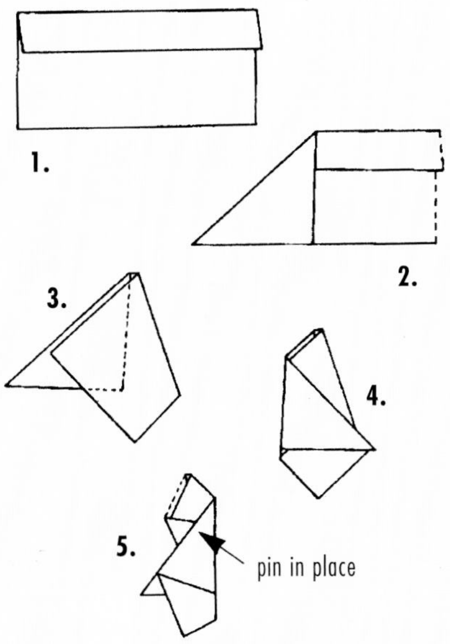

FINISHED SIZE

- Finished quilt size is approximately 65cm (26in) square.

MATERIALS

- 50cm (20in) square fabric for the background
- 50cm (20in) square of two different green fabrics for the leaves
- 20cm (¼yd) each of ten different fabrics for the flowers, ranging in value
- Variety of fabric scraps for centres of daisies
- 20cm (¼yd) fabric for the inner border
- 50cm (⅝yd) fabric for the outer border
- 40cm (½yd) fabric for the binding
- 70cm (28in) square of Pellon or low-loft batting
- 70cm (28in) square of backing fabric
- 20cm (¼yd) of Vliesofix
- Thread to match fabrics
- Buttons for flower centres (optional)
- Template plastic
- HB or white pencil
- Sewing machine
- Spray starch

NOTE: All fabrics must be pre-washed and pressed.

Diagram 1
Inner Petals for Daisy.

1. Fold the top down a quarter of the distance. Finger-press.
2. Fold half of the left side of the rectangle over.
3. Fold the other half over, leaving a ⅛in gap at the centre top then fold to run ⅛in parallel to the left fold.
4. Measure ½in down the left edge, fold from this point from left to right at an angle.
5. Measure ½in down the right edge and fold from this point right to left at an angle. Pin in place and carefully trim excess fabric. Secure with a stitch.

Constructing the yoyo flowers and the daisy petals.

PUFFED FLOWERS

Using Template 1, choose two fabrics and trace five of each for the petals and cut them out. Stitch ⅛in from the raw edge and pull up tightly and secure.

Place five petals in a circle and stitch in place. Using Template 6, make a yoyo for the centre of the puffed flower following the directions for the centre of the daisy. Stitch in place.

RUCHED FLOWERS

The large and small flowers are worked in the same way. The only difference is the length of fabric.

For the large flower, cut a 2in strip of fabric from selvedge to selvedge. Press down ½in on both long sides. With a long stitch on your machine, zigzag along the length of the strip at repeated right angles (see Diagram 2). Pull gently to gather, or ruche. Fold the beginning of the strip under to hide the raw edges.

Place this piece on top then twist the remainder around in a circle, finishing underneath the last row. Secure with a stitch on each petal formed. Tuck end under. Repeat for the smaller flower, only this time cut the strip 31½in long.

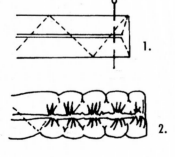

Diagram 2
Ruched flowers.

1. Take the 2in strip and fold the two edges in ½in to meet in the centre. Zigzag a long stitch along the length of the strip.
2. Pull gently to gather. Fold beginning of strip under to hide raw edges.
3. Place this on top, twist remainder around in a circle, underneath the last row. Secure with a stitch on each petal. Tuck end under.

The flowers are now ready to be placed on the block.

SEWING

Fold and finger-press the background square into quarters to establish the centre of the block. Using the photograph as a guide, place the leaves in position and press onto the background fabric. Zigzag stitch through the centre.

Place the flowers on the block. The arrangement will depend on your fabric and the visual appearance. Pin and stitch them in place by hand with a slip stitch, or use a short straight stitch on the machine.

For the foliage at the base of the flowers, cut five strips of different greens 20in x 3in wide. Follow the instructions for the ruched flowers. Instead of coiling the strip, simply twist it. Stitch into position. Decorate the flowers with decorative buttons, including birds, butterflies and a frog.

BORDERS

Cut four strips 28in x 1½in for the inner border and four strips measuring 28in x 4in for the outer border.

Sew the sides of the inner border to the quilt top first and press the seam allowances towards the outside. Stitch the top and the bottom, trim and press.

Repeat the steps for the outer border.

QUILTING

Place the backing fabric, batting and finished block on top. Baste. Stipple quilt on the background square around and among the leaves and flowers, taking great care not to catch the petals. The outer border is also stipple quilted.

FINISHING

BINDING

Cut four strips of fabric measuring 28in x 3in. Fold them in half with wrong sides together and press.

Sew the sides of the quilt first, then sew the top and bottom through all layers. Fold the binding towards the back of the quilt and slip stitch right around the edge to secure.

Make a label for the the back and sign and date your quilt.

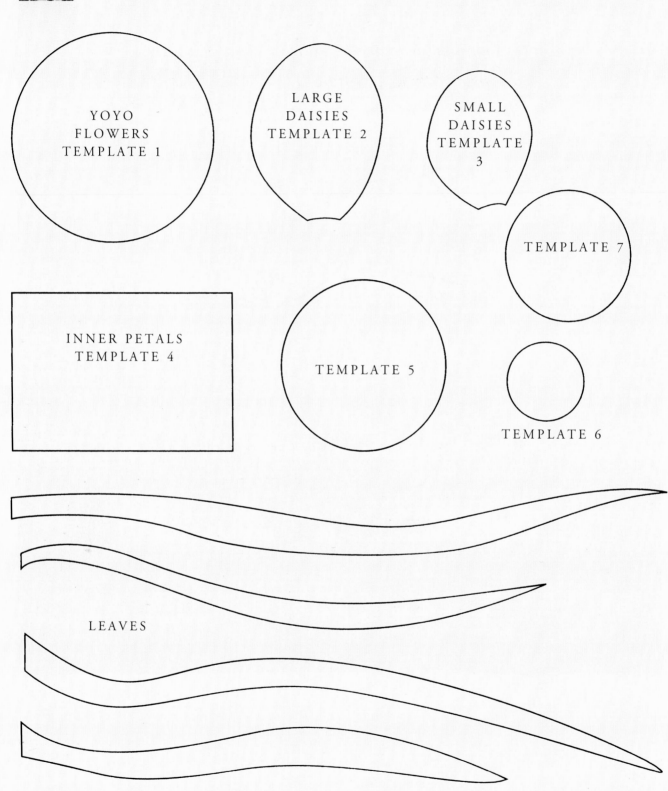

YOYO
FLOWERS
TEMPLATE 1

LARGE
DAISIES
TEMPLATE 2

SMALL
DAISIES
TEMPLATE
3

TEMPLATE 7

INNER PETALS
TEMPLATE 4

TEMPLATE 5

TEMPLATE 6

LEAVES

105%

Naive Appliqué Flannel Quilt

*Warm flannels and country cottons
are combined with naive appliqué to create a quilt
that's as cuddly as it is cute. The appliqué shapes
are attached using the fusible webbing method.*

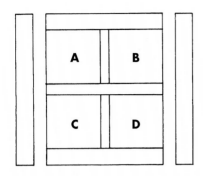

Diagram 1
Sew together the four centre blocks using the joining strips and add the first narrow strip border.

Below left: Cut out the shapes and iron them into position on the background fabric.

Below right: Buttonhole stitch over the raw edges.

PREPARATION

CUTTING

Appliquéd Centre and Border
From the plain flannel, cut two strips (along the selvedge) 45½in x 6½in wide; two strips (along the selvedge) 33½in x 6½in wide; and four 8in squares for the centre appliqué. Set the remainder aside for the binding.

The appliqué shapes are attached using the fusible webbing method. Trace the appropriate designs for the centre blocks onto the paper side of the fusible webbing. Iron the webbing, adhesive side down, to the wrong side of the fabric scraps. Cut out the shapes, peel off the backing paper and iron (fuse) in place on the 8in squares. Blanket stitch around all the raw edges of the appliqué pieces using two strands of black thread.

Embroider the mouth and nose onto the little girls. Using six strands of embroidery thread, tie into knots across the top of the heads, leaving ¼in to ½in ends for the hair. Fuse the door and windows to the house and blanket stitch

around all the raw edges. Embroider the comb, eyes, legs and flowers onto the chicken block.

Fuse the houses, trees, flowers and hearts to the border pieces, referring to the photograph for placement, and blanket stitch around all the raw edges.

Centre Joining Strips and First Border
From the check flannel, cut two pieces 16½in x 3in; two pieces 21½in x 3in; one piece 16½in x 1½in; and two pieces 8in x 1½in.

Sew a short joining strip 8in x 1½in between A and B centre blocks (see Diagram 1) and between C and D centre blocks. Next, sew the long joining strip, 16½in x 1½in between these two sections. Press the seams away from the appliqué.

Add the two short borders, press towards the border, then add the two long borders.

Nine-patch Border
Cut six 1½in wide strips from the two dark and two light flannels.

Using an exact ¼in seam allowance, sew two dark strips with one light strip together and two light strips with one

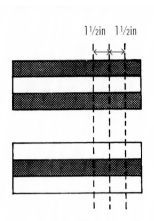

Diagram 2
Join the strips in sets of three, then cross-cut into 1½in strips.

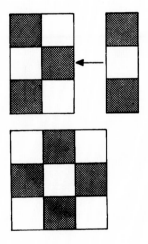

Diagram 3
Join the pieced strips to make two opposing Nine-patch blocks.

dark strip together (see Diagram 2). Iron the seams towards the dark fabric and cross-cut into 1½in sections. Assemble into a block (see Diagram 3), matching all seams. Make sixteen blocks with five dark and four light squares of fabric, and sixteen blocks with five light and four dark squares of fabric. The shorter borders are made up of seven blocks sewn together, the longer borders are made up of nine blocks sewn together. Attach the borders, referring to the photograph for placement.

ASSEMBLY

Cut the remaining flannels and cottons into 2in wide strips to make up the pieced and narrow strip borders. Use these 2in strips to add two contrasting borders around the Nine-patch border.

Attach the appliqué border, followed by another two strip borders. The last pieced border is made up of 2in wide x 7in long strips of fabric, sewn together. Join pieces to make two borders 51½in long x 7in wide, and two borders of 64½in long x 7in wide. Again, attach the shorter sides first.

BACKING

Cut about 85cm off the length of the backing fabric. Cut this piece in half to give two pieces 57cm x 85cm. Sew these together along the 57cm side. Sew this piece to the remaining 165cm of backing fabric (see Diagram 4). Cut and join the batting down the centre with a large herringbone stitch.

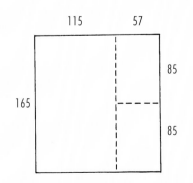

Diagram 4
Cut and join the backing fabric.

FINISHED SIZE

- Finished quilt size is approximately 64½in (163cm) square.

MATERIALS

- 1.5m (1¾yd) plain flannel for centre blocks and appliqué border
- 30cm (⅓yd) each of four different flannels for Nine-patch border (two dark and two light)
- 30cm (⅓yd) dark check flannel for first border and centre joining strips
- 25cm (10in) each of three different flannels for strip and pieced borders (these can be checks, stripes or prints)
- Assorted cotton scraps for appliqué and to mix in through the quilt.
- 1.5m (1¾yd) fusible webbing
- 3.3m of 90cm (3¾yd of 36in) wide Pellon or similar low loft batting
- 2.5m of 115cm (2¾yd of 45in) wide fabric for backing.
- 1 skein Coton Perlé thread for tying
- 2 skeins black embroidery thread for Blanket Stitch edging on appliqué
- Assorted embroidery threads
- Thirty-six small buttons
- Rotary cutter, mat and ruler
- Sewing machine and thread

NOTE: Cutting instructions include ¼in (6mm) seam allowance. This quilt has easy squared corners. Sew the short borders to the centre first, then the longer borders. The appliqué and Nine-patch borders are completed first, then the quilt is assembled with the remaining fabric scraps.

STITCHES USED

Blanket Stitch, Back Stitch

Herringbone Stitch

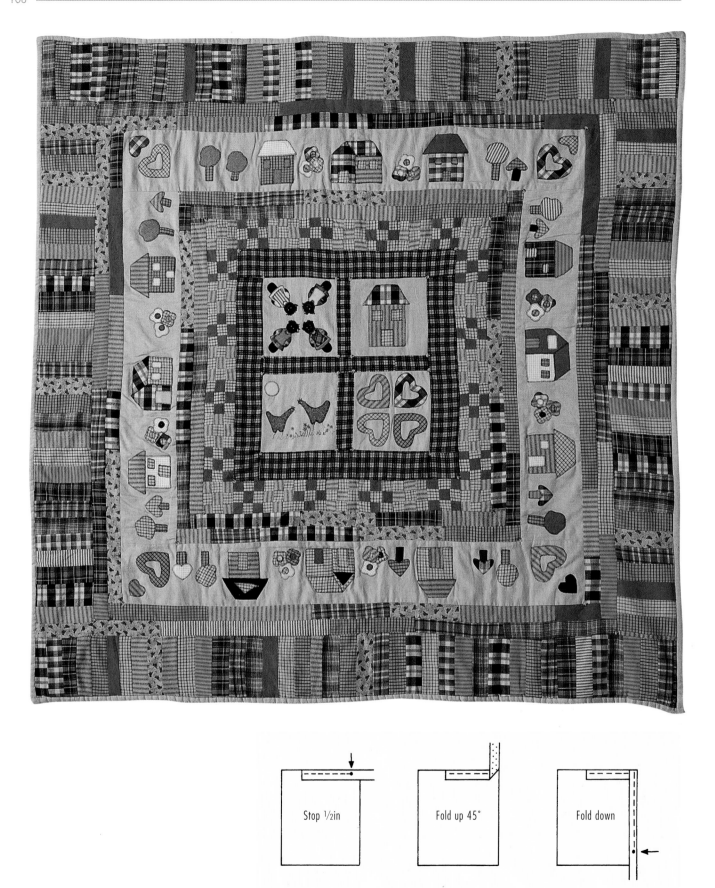

Diagram 5
Mitre the binding.

Stop ½in

Fold up 45°

Fold down

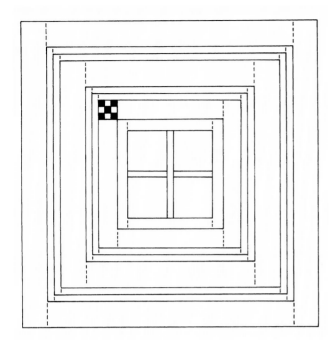

Layout Diagram, showing the placement of the borders.

The appliqué detail on the centre panel.

FINISHING

Sandwich the backing fabric, batting and quilt top together and baste or pin it in place. Sew buttons into the corners of the centre block and also on each set of borders.

TYING

The quilt should be tied on the back, approximately every 6in, using Coton Perlé thread. To make a tie, hold the needle at right angles to the quilt, push the needle down through all thicknesses of the quilt and back up about ⅛in away, tie a reef knot and cut about ½in from the knot.

To make a reef knot, take the left thread over the right thread, under and pull, then take the right over the left, under and pull. This is also known as a square knot and can be done twice if needed.

BINDING

Trim the edges of the quilt. Cut five 3in strips along the whole length of the remaining plain flannel. Prepare the binding by sewing these strips into a continuous strip. Press, with wrong sides together, in half along the length of the strip. Starting at the centre bottom of the quilt, sew the binding to the quilt top with all raw edges together ½in from the edge.

To mitre the binding, stop ½in from the corner, back stitch, then take the binding out of the machine. Fold the binding up, making a 45 degree angle, then fold it down level with the quilt edge. Pin, then sew along the edge of the quilt to the next corner and repeat (see Diagram 5). Overlap the ends of the binding, turn them to the back and slip stitch them in place.

Make a label for the back and sign and date your quilt.

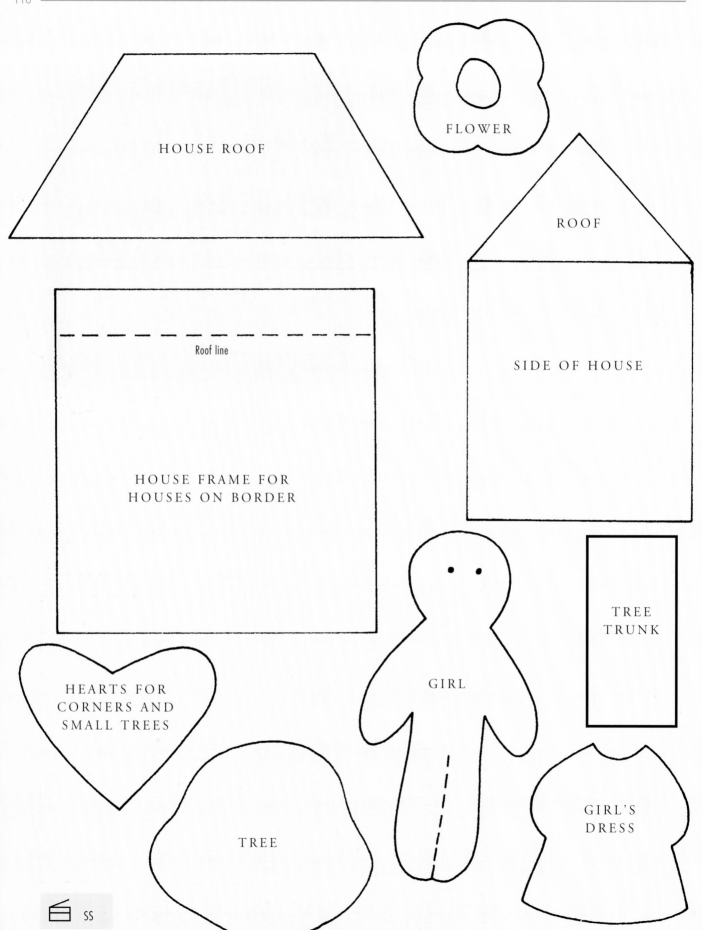

HOUSE ROOF

FLOWER

ROOF

Roof line

SIDE OF HOUSE

HOUSE FRAME FOR
HOUSES ON BORDER

TREE
TRUNK

HEARTS FOR
CORNERS AND
SMALL TREES

GIRL

TREE

GIRL'S
DRESS

SS

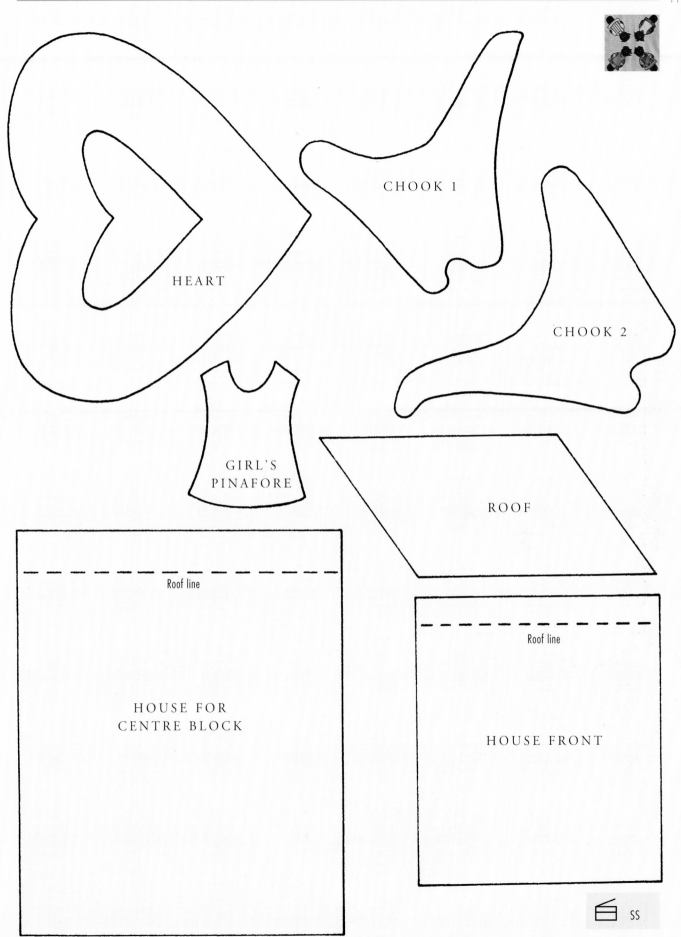

HEART

CHOOK 1

CHOOK 2

GIRL'S
PINAFORE

ROOF

Roof line

HOUSE FOR
CENTRE BLOCK

Roof line

HOUSE FRONT

SS

Penny Rugg

Quilters of yesteryear made Penny Ruggs from woollen scraps.
The word 'rugg' actually referred to a woollen bed cover which was decorated
with floral motifs and sewn with a blanket stitch or herringbone stitch.
This type of rugg was used to decorate the tops of tables or chests.

PREPARATION

Fold the square of background felt to find the centre. Trace the appliqué shapes provided onto freezer paper (don't cut the shapes out) and iron the freezer paper onto the appropriate fabric. Cut out the shapes – it is much easier to cut through the paper and felt, rather than cutting out the freezer paper shapes first.

CONSTRUCTION

Position the shapes on the background and blanket stitch around all the shapes using two strands of the gold embroidery thread. Chain stitch the veins on the leaves also using two strands of thread.

Work the legs on the birds in stem stitch in two strands of thread.

Cut fifty-six large and fifty-six small circles. Buttonhole the small circles to large circles before attaching the large circles to the background.

FINISHING

BACKING

Turn under the edges of the completed felt quilt top, ½in on all sides and baste them down. Turn under the edges of the black homespun backing fabric ½in on all sides and baste them down. Place the backing and the top wrong sides together and slip stitch right around the edges using the chenille needle and the black thread.

FINISHED SIZE

• Finished quilt size is 53.5cm (21in) square.

MATERIALS

• 56cm (22in) square of black fabric for the background

• 56cm (22in) square of black homespun for the backing

• 13cm (5in) square of deep red fabric for the flower

• 23cm (9in) square of soft blue-green fabric for the leaves

• 21cm (8in) square of beige fabric for the birds

• Scraps of charcoal blue fabric for the tulips

• Scraps of yellow fabric for the centre of the star

• 46cm x 77cm (18in x 30in) of deep red fabric for the large circles

• 46cm x 61cm (18in x 24in) of charcoal blue fabric for the small circles

• Freezer paper

• Gold embroidery thread

• Chenille needle Size 18 or 20

• Black thread

You can use 100 per cent woollen fabric for this project or take advantage of the wonderful antique coloured felts that are available (this is good quality felt not craft squares). If you are using old woollen clothing, you can felt the fabric yourself by washing it in very hot water, then placing it in the clothes dryer. If you are using brand new woollen fabric, don't feel guilty. You would happily throw brand new cotton fabric into tea for an instantly old effect! These rugs look wonderful when combined as a decorating tool with the popular flannel quilts. Make yours any shape you like.

STITCHES USED

Blanket Stitch, Chain Stitch

Herringbone Stitch

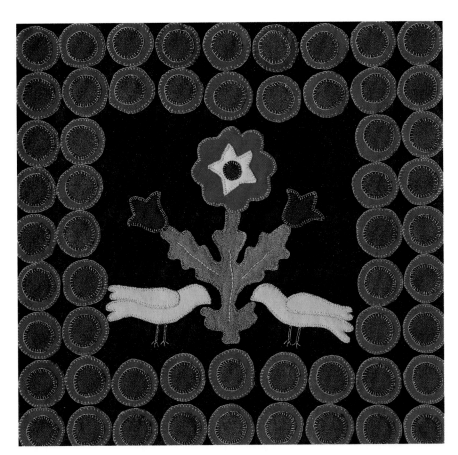

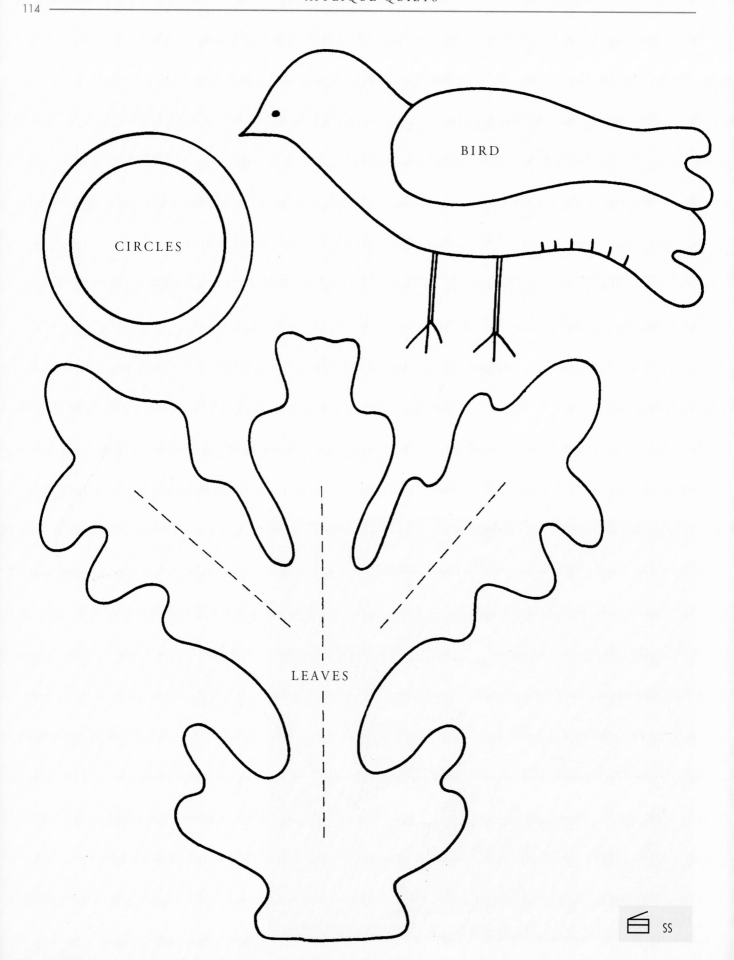

CIRCLES

BIRD

LEAVES

SS

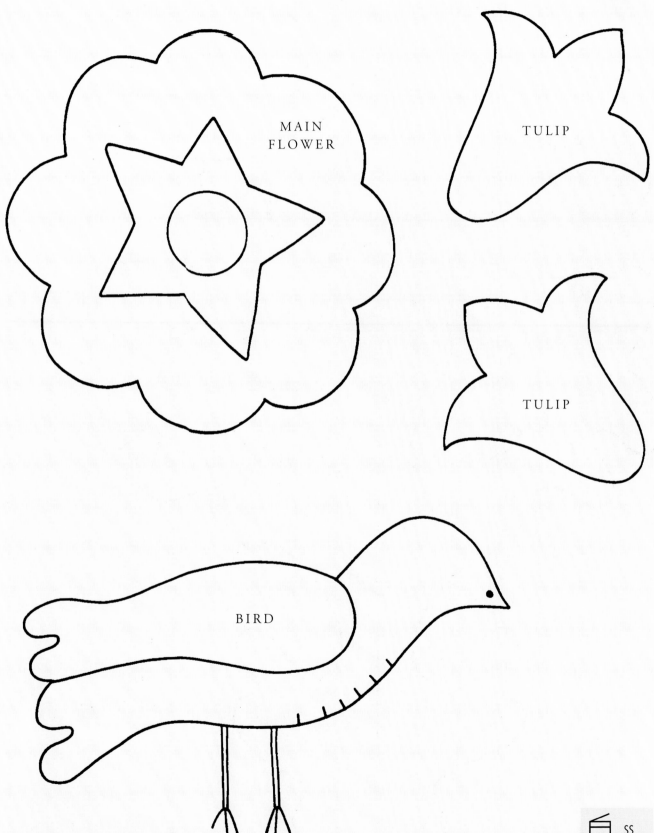

MAIN
FLOWER

TULIP

TULIP

BIRD

SS

Serenity

This beautiful quilt features a reverse appliqué design which is worked with the background fabrics on top of the design fabrics. The shapes are cut out of the background fabric. Busy floral prints form the three borders.

TECHNIQUES AND TERMS

Appliqué: Is the fixing down of a chosen shape onto a background fabric for decoration or repair.

Reverse Appliqué: Is worked with the background fabrics placed on top of the design fabrics and the shapes are cut out of the background. The remaining edges are then sewn down onto the design fabric.

Hawaiian Appliqué: Is not reverse appliqué. For this type of appliqué the design is cut from one large folded piece of fabric, opened out and spread on top of the background then sewn down. Some small sections within the design may be cut and sewn in the same way as reverse appliqué, but the background remains underneath.

NOTE: All forms of appliqué use the same basic sewing stitch.

The Appliqué Stitch: Use your needle to turn the edge of the fabric under. Hold it in place with the thumb against the finger beneath. You can use a pin or two placed at right angles to the fold just ahead of the stitching. Move the pins along as you proceed. Use thread to match the fabric being folded and begin with a small knot at the back.

Bring the needle up again no more than 1/8in to the left of the previous stitch and repeat.

Diagram 1
The Appliqué Stitch

Work from right to left with the fold facing upwards. Begin on a straight or slightly curved section, never at a corner or point. Bring the needle up through both fabrics into the fold of the top fabric, then down through the bottom fabric immediately near the fold and as close as possible to where the thread comes out of the fold. Come up again no more than 1/8in to the left of the previous stitch and repeat (see Diagram 1).

NOTE: Stitches would normally be no more than 1/8in apart and even closer at points and tight curves. Smooth the edge carefully as you go – what you fold is what you sew and it is permanent. Work the edge with your needle until you are satisfied with its shape.

As you sew, snip and remove the marking thread after folding the edge, or be sure it is out of sight under the fold.

In the Vs, or indents, snip to within two or three threads of the point and use very small, close stitches as the turnover will be very narrow.

On the points, slip the needle tip between the two fabrics and bring it two or three threads beyond the point. Put the needle down at the point and up close by to make the next small stitch. Stitches will show at these points; it is unavoidable. Just be sure to match your thread closely to the fabric.

FINISHED SIZE

- Finished size is 33in x 36½in (84cm x 93cm) approximately.

MATERIALS

- 1.3m (1½yd) finely woven, non-transparent 100 per cent cotton background fabric
- 1m (1⅛yd) floral print for borders (this should be an all-over busy floral)
- 13 strips of fabric, cut 4cm x 57cm (1½in x 22in) in colours ranging from dark to light, including at least one strip of the border print fabric
- 90cm (1yd) cotton fabric for backing
- 89cm x 97cm (35in x 38in) piece of thin batting
- Thread to match background fabric, contrasting thread for basting, one skein of stranded embroidery thread to match background colour
- Size 10 or 12 appliqué needles (sharps)
- H or HB pencil, chalk or silver pencil
- Sewing machine and sewing supplies

NOTE: The appliqué and border design will need to be enlarged by 200 per cent on a photocopier. Before commencing this project it is important to read all the instructions.

STITCHES USED

Stem Stitch, Satin Stitch
Appliqué Stitch

background fabric on top

design fabric

cutting line

basted line marking finished edge

seam allowance

Remember the seam allowance is cut inside the marked shape.

Diagram 2

At the outer corners or points, stitch up to the corner and make an extra stitch at the tip. Turn the next edge under with the needle, smoothing the edge to a neat shape and continue stitching.

CONSTRUCTION

Cut a piece of background fabric, 22in x 26in and overcast the edges to prevent it fraying (see the background fabric cutting chart on the Pattern Sheet). Press the background smooth then fold in four and press lightly to mark the centre. Baste the fold lines with a contrasting thread.

Sew the thirteen strips together in your planned order using ¼in seams. Press all the seams in one direction.

Trace the enlarged printed design and tape the tracing to a lightbox or window with the printed side up. Tape the piece of background fabric over the design, with the wrong side up, matching the centre point and guide lines. This will reverse the design on the finished quilt – it is planned this way. Using an H or HB pencil, trace all lines onto the fabric, including the border lines and designs – you will need to reposition the fabric and reverse the corner designs on two of the corners to complete this. Use a ruler to draw the outer line.

NOTE: The solid lines represent the areas to be reverse appliquéd, the broken lines represent the embroidery. The round centres of the small flowers are added once the reverse appliqué is complete.

Using a contrasting thread, baste along all the marked lines with ¼in to ½in stitches to transfer the pattern to the right side of the fabric.

Tape the design piece (the joined strips) to the lightbox or window with the strips running from top to bottom. Tape the background fabric, with right side up, over the top of the design piece, aligning the seams in the design piece parallel with the vertical guide line on the background fabric. Ensure that the design area is covered by the strip piece, but it need not extend to the oval shaped border. Pin the background securely to the design piece. Lay it flat and baste around the edge of the design area and between the larger areas of the design.

Beginning with a large area near the centre, such as the large tulip petal, carefully lift the layers apart and snip a small hole ¼in inside the tulip shape. Remember the seam allowance is cut INSIDE the marked shape (see Diagram 2).

Cut ¼in inside the marked line for about one inch, through the top layer only, then begin stitching. Cut only one or two inches ahead at a time to reduce fraying and distortion of the shape. Complete the design area, working out from the centre. Press the design area only when all the appliqué is finished.

To make the small flower centres, trace the circle from the enlarged pattern onto a scrap of greeting card or similar and cut it out carefully. Cut out a 1in circle of background fabric and run a gathering thread ⅛in in from the edge. Place the card circle on the reverse side of the fabric and pull the gathers over it to form a neat circle. For added texture add a small piece of batting between the card and the fabric circle. Appliqué the completed circle in the centre of the flower, carefully matching the grainlines. There is no need to remove such a small piece of card.

The embroidery can now be added. Fill the larger petal shapes with satin stitch or your preferred filling stitch. Use two or three strands of thread in a matching colour to stem stitch in the remaining design. Press the work lightly with a warm iron.

OVAL BORDER

Trim the joined design piece back to ¼in over the inner oval border line. The pieces which are cut off can be used to reverse appliqué the small flowers in the corners (see the printed border fabric cutting chart on the Pattern Sheet).

Trace the quarter oval design from the enlarged pattern twice onto white paper and cut out. Fold the 12in x 45in border fabric in half, place the enlarged pattern for the border on top and cut out, adding ½in seam allowance all around. Join the narrow ends with ½in seam allowance to make the oval shape. Press the seams open, taking care not to stretch the edges. Place the quilt top right side down on the table, lay the oval right side down on top, covering the marked oval. It should extend ½in on both sides, if not, it may be necessary to adjust the seams. Baste in place ¼in each side of the marked oval. Reverse appliqué in place from the front of the quilt. Trim the seam allowance back to ¼in.

Check that the quilt has not been distorted by the appliqué at this stage, using the marked line as a guide. Re-mark as necessary and trim edges allowing for ¼in seams.

RECTANGULAR BORDER

Measure from the top to the bottom of the quilt at the centre. Cut two 1½in strips of print fabric to this length and sew them to the sides of the quilt with ¼in seams. Press the seams towards the quilt. Repeat for the top and bottom borders, measuring across the quilt at the centre.

WIDE BORDER

Cut four 5½in strips of background fabric and attach the remaining two strips of fabric to the top and bottom. If you are using a chintz fabric it may be advisable to mitre the corners to

avoid an obvious change in shading due to the change in direction of the fabric.

QUILTING

This quilt is outline-quilted around all the design and borders and ditch quilted in the seam lines of the strips extending to the oval border. On the wide border elements of the appliqué design are repeated, slightly smaller in size. Mark the border quilting design with chalk or a silver pencil. Layer the backing, batting and quilt top and baste or pin them together. Quilt in a hoop or frame. Trim the edges leaving ¼in seam.

FINISHING

Cut four of the floral print fabric strips 4¾in wide for the binding. Press these strips in half and sew them to the sides first, checking the measurements across the quilt as you did for the borders. Fold them to the back and hand stitch them in place. Repeat for the top and bottom binding measuring from the top to the bottom of the quilt at the centre first. Finish the ends neatly, or mitre them if preferred.

Make a rod sleeve or loops and attach them to the back of the quilt for hanging.

Make a label for the back and sign and date your quilt.

117% then 200%

Whirling Flowers Table Quilt

The fashionable colours of the 1930s
have been used to create this elegant table cover.
The appliquéd flowers are cut from bright
reproduction pastels of this era.

FINISHED SIZE

- Finished quilt size is 150cm (59in) square.

MATERIALS

- Extra-wide ivory homespun for background, minimum 150cm (60in) square
- 60cm (⅝yd) plain for solid bands (green) and binding
- 35cm (⅜yd) small floral (daisy) border
- Range of bright 1930s-look fabrics for flowers
- 10cm (⅛yd) yellow for flower centres
- 1.8m (2yd) backing fabric
- 180cm (70in) approx. square of batting
- Matching threads
- Template plastic and lightweight cardboard
- Spray starch
- Water-soluble marking pen

STITCHES USED

Slip Stitch

The traditional or English method of appliqué has been used in this design. You may prefer, however, to stitch with the method of appliqué you are more familiar with, such as needle-turn or freezer-paper techniques.

PREPARATION

❖

TRADITIONAL APPLIQUE

Trace the petal pattern and the centre circle from the pattern provided onto template plastic and cut out carefully, smoothing the curved edges. Use the template to trace the petal pattern onto lightweight cardboard and cut out on the lines with no jagged edges on your paper. The quilt requires one hundred petals and twenty centres.

Place the cardboard petal shape face down on the back of the bright floral fabric and pin it in place.

Cut out the required number of petals and centres, allowing ¼in seam allowance all around as you cut.

CONSTRUCTION

❖

PETALS

Using needle and thread, fold the seam allowance firmly over the edge of the cardboard template and baste through the fabric and cardboard. As you baste the seam allowance into place you will need to make small tucks to ease the fullness. You may have to clip the curves as you go. Check the right side as you stitch to see that the work is smooth and firm (see step-by-step photograph).

CENTRES

Work a row of running stitches in the seam allowance, about the centre of

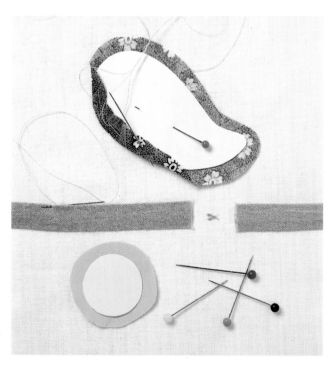

Baste fabric for appliqué onto cardboard templates. Mark positions for flowers and appliqué green bands first.

Flower petals positioned around the X mark, ready to be appliquéd. The yellow centre is added last.

the raw edge. Draw in the thread around the template and tie off the ends.

Press the petals and centres firmly with the iron and use spray starch to keep the seam allowances in place. When you are ready to position the piece to be appliquéd, remove the basting, carefully ease out the cardboard to keep in shape, then pin it in place using the flower placement pattern as a guide.

Colour-match your thread to the appliquéd piece as close as possible. Using a small appliqué needle, stitch in place using a hidden slip stitch.

QUILT BACKGROUND

Remove the selvedge and square off your fabric to 59in square. Fold the fabric in half, then in half again. Press with an iron to find the centre and mark this with the blue water-soluble marking pen.

To mark the placement onto your background, refer to Quilt Construction Diagram provided on page 124.

Using the centre point, measure and mark 4in each way to make an 8in square for the middle (A) flowers. Mark four As.

Go to the outside edge on each corner of the fabric and measure in 10in

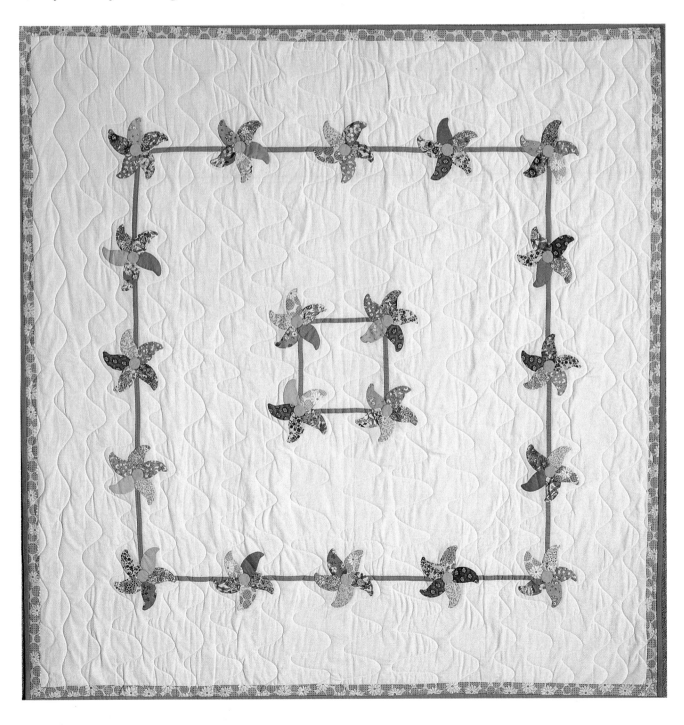

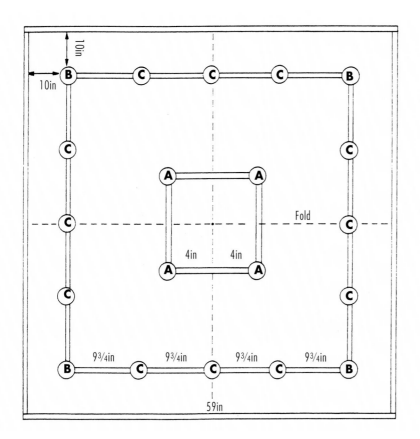

Quilt Construction Diagram

as shown on the diagram. Mark (B) position in four corners.

Mark in a straight line from corner B to B at intervals of 9¾in, these will be marked as (C). Flowers will be centred around these marks.

Before stitching the flowers, appliqué the plain fabric strips (the bands placed behind the flowers).

These bands are made by cutting straight strips of green fabric, 1⅛in wide. They can be stitched and pressed over a ⅜in bias bar if you have one.

Alternatively, press each side under as if making bias binding. Baste the bands in place, making sure you keep them very straight.

Position the joins of these strips of fabric so that each one is concealed under the flowers.

Appliqué the bands in place, using a matching thread and a hidden slip stitch (see step-by-step photograph).

When you have covered and pressed all the flower shapes and centres, place the flowers on the A, B and C positions. Refer to the pattern and photograph for placement of the flowers.

Select the fabric petals in a pleasing combination for each flower and overlap the petals in the one direction, to give them a whirling effect.

Baste or pin the flowers and petals in position, then appliqué them. Complete each flower with a yellow centre (see step-by-step photograph).

BORDER

When all the appliqué is completed, add the daisy border. Cut eight strips, 1½in wide across the width of the fabric. Join the strips in pairs to make the lengths to the required size. Attach strips to the opposite sides, trim to length, then attach to the top and bottom of the quilt.

ASSEMBLY AND QUILTING

When all the appliqué is completed, press the quilt top. Lay out the backing, batting and quilt top. Baste or pin together, working closely from the centre out to the edges.

Quilt by hand or machine as desired. The featured quilt is machine-quilted with an irregular wave pattern.

FINISHING

BINDING

Straighten and trim the edges if necessary. Cut six binding strips 2½in wide across the fabric width, press in half lengthways, wrong sides together.

With the binding on top and matching raw edges, sew to the two opposite sides using ¼in seam. Fold to the back and pin in place. Sew binding to the two other sides, leaving ¼in extra at each end. Neatly fold in the ends, fold the binding to the back and slip stitch all sides and corners.

Make a label for the back and sign and date your quilt.

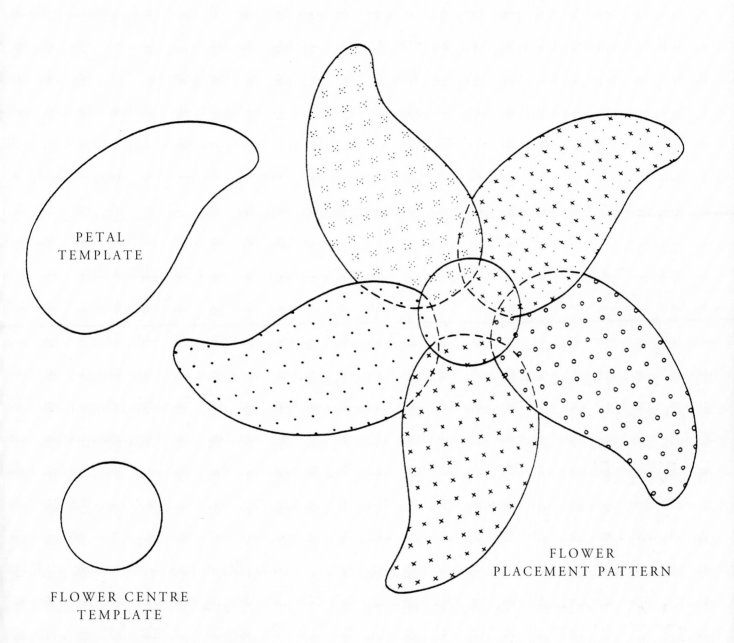

PETAL
TEMPLATE

FLOWER CENTRE
TEMPLATE

FLOWER
PLACEMENT PATTERN

Sweet Dreams

*Most of us who make quilts do so because they are a way of making
our house a home. We make them to provide warmth — both physical
and emotional, for the ones we love or for those in need.
Dreams are always sweeter when we can snuggle up under quilts
such as the ones displayed on the following pages.*

Floral Wreath Quilt

*Based on a block known as the President's Wreath,
this pretty quilt can be made to any size
by repeating the block, or make only one
as a wall-hanging or cushion.*

PREPARATION

❖

CUTTING

Trace the patterns from the Pattern Sheet onto the template plastic. There is a large flower, inner flower, calyx, flower centre and leaf.

From the background fabric, cut six 18½in background squares and four 10in border strips down the remaining length of the fabric (approximately 1.75m).

To mark the pattern on the background squares, fold each square in half both ways and crease the centre lines. Place the square over the pattern and trace the design onto the fabric using an HB pencil. Draw just inside the design lines, so that the pencil marks are covered by the appliqué.

Prepare bias stems by cutting several 1in strips on the bias. Press each strip right side out, in half, to give a length of bias that is ½in wide.

✄ HELPFUL HINT

For appliqué the needle should enter the background fabric directly opposite where it came out on the top piece and slightly under the piece being appliquéd.

CONSTRUCTION

❖

NOTE: Sewing thread should match the fabric being appliquéd.

Sew the bias stems to the background by placing the raw edges of the bias on the inside curve of the stem line. Pin them in place. Trim the ends of the bias leaving ½in to go under where the flower will be positioned. Sew this bias stem into position using a small running stitch, one-third of the way in from the raw edges. Roll the bias stem over the stitching line to cover the raw edges. Pin the stem into place and appliqué down using a blind stitch. Complete all four stems on the block.

Prepare the required number of flowers, leaves and calyx for the block. Using an HB or white pencil, draw around the template onto the right side of the fabric. Cut out the individual shapes, leaving a lean ¼in seam allowance.

Some leaves are reversed, so turn the template over to trace these.

Using the pencil line as a guide, turn the seam allowance under and baste. You will need to snip almost to the pencil line on the inverted points of the flowers and calyx.

FINISHED SIZE

- Finished quilt size is approximately 160cm x 210cm (63in x 83in).

MATERIALS

NOTE: Materials are based on 112cm (45in) wide fabric

- 3.25m (3½yd) background fabric
- 1m (1⅛yd) fabric for large flower, flower centre and folded buds
- 1.2m (1⅓yd) fabric for small inner flower and binding
- 1.2m (1⅓yd) fabric for stems and leaves
- 70cm (¾yd) fabric for calyx, dark leaves and sashing squares
- 80cm (⅞yd) fabric for sashing
- 4.5m (5yd) backing fabric
- 78cm x 98cm (166in x 216in) batting
- Threads to match all appliqué fabrics
- HB pencil (or white pencil if working with dark fabrics)
- H pencil for marking quilting designs
- Template plastic
- Quilting thread (for hand quilting)

STITCHES USED

Running Stitch, Blind Appliqué Stitch

Draw around the templates and cut out with a lean ¼in seam.

Using the pencil line as a guide, baste the flowers, leaves and bias stems.

Appliqué the stems, flowers and leaves to the background square.

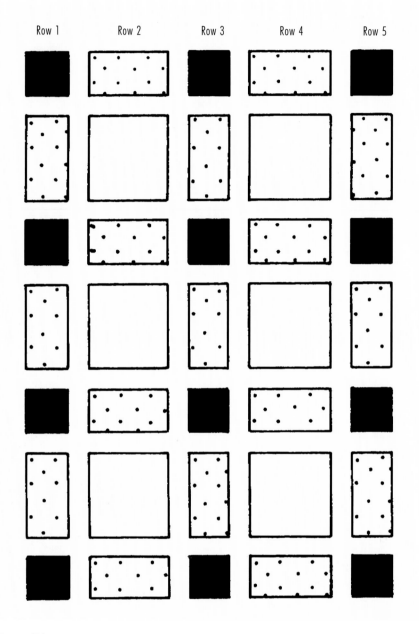

Row 1	Row 2	Row 3	Row 4	Row 5

Layout Diagram

Prepare the folded buds by cutting four 1½in squares. Fold each square diagonally to form a triangle. Fold both of the points of the triangle to the square corner and press. The raw edges will sit under the calyx leaving the bud tip free.

Place the large flowers into position on the background square, with the fullness of the petals covering the ends of the bias stems. Pin and appliqué in place. Sew extra stitches in the inverted point. Place the inner flowers and leaves in position and appliqué. Pin the calyx onto the background and appliqué from point to point. Insert the folded bud into the opening, pin and continue to appliqué. Try to stitch through all layers.

For the flower centres, make a cardboard template of the centre circle. Mark around the template on the wrong side of the fabric and cut out leaving a generous ¼in seam allowance. Sew a small running stitch halfway between the drawn line and the raw edge. Place the cardboard template on the wrong side and gather the thread around the cardboard. Tie the ends of the threads. Press this circle, then ease the cardboard out to use again. Now appliqué the centres on the flowers. Remove all the basting, then press the completed block on the wrong side using a medium to hot steam iron.

Make six blocks in total.

ASSEMBLY

For the sashings, cut nine 2¾in strips across the fabric and from each strip, cut two 18½in sections.

For the sashing squares, cut one 2¾in strip across the leaf fabric and from this, cut twelve 2¾in squares.

Piece the sashing, squares and blocks together to form vertical rows (see Layout Diagram) using ¼in seam allowance.

Press all seams towards the sashings.

Sew the borders to the quilt, sewing the sides first then the top and bottom. Press all the seams out.

Mark the border design by tracing the large flower at each sashing square around the border leaving a 1in space between the seam and flower. Mark another flower halfway between each two flowers leaving 1½in space between the flower and the edge of the quilt. Draw the stems freehand between the flowers to create the curved design. Place three leaves on each curved stem.

Appliqué the stems, flowers and leaves using the same methods as the appliqué for the blocks.

Alternatively, make a pattern for one of the scallop units, then trace onto the borders for consistent placing.

FINISHING

Trace the quilt designs from the Pattern Sheet onto the top using an H pencil. Make backing by cutting fabric length in half and joining together to fit quilt tip.

Sandwich the quilt top, batting and backing together and baste with a grid of approximately 6in. Quilt by hand or machine, working from the centre out.

Shape the edges if desired by laying the quilt on a flat surface, and work from the centre of the side of the quilt to the centre of the top or bottom. Make a paper template with gentle curves shaping up into the flowers and out around the stems. This paper template can be used on each corner of the quilt to mark the cutting line.

To bind the quilt, cut 2¼in strips on the bias, join together and press in half along the length of the binding. Start sewing on a straight section, matching the raw edges of the binding to the raw edges of the quilt, and attaching

the binding to the right side of the quilt. Leave a 2in tail and sew with a ¼in seam. As the inverted point is reached, stop the machine, leave the needle down, pivot the quilt and continue sewing the binding down the next curve. When the beginning is reached, stop about 2in from the tail. Take the quilt from the machine and carefully join and pin the ends. Trim any excess binding and sew. Turn the binding to the back of the quilt and slip stitch by hand.

Make a label for the back and sign and date your quilt.

Peonies Forever

*This quilt was named after the traditional
Double Peony block and for the length of time
it took the quilter to complete it.
It is the perfect long-term project for hand piecing.*

Hand piecing requires precisely marked seam lines, however marked cutting lines are optional. To mark the patches, place the template face down on the wrong side of the fabric and draw around it with a sharp pencil. Leave enough space between patches for an approximate ¼in (6mm) seam allowance.

Cut out the patches, measuring the seam allowance by eye. Because the patches are pieced with right sides together, the marked seam line on the wrong side of the fabric will be visible on both sides when you are stitching.

Using a single thread, sew the seam through the pencilled line with a short running stitch and an occasional back stitch. Begin and end each seam at the seam line (not at the edge of the fabric) with two or three back stitches to secure the seam.

NOTE: Sew only from point to point, not edge to edge.

When you are joining the blocks and rows together, take care not to sew the seam allowance down. Instead, sew right up to the dot marking the corner, then begin on the next side of the block by again taking a couple of small back stitches and continue sewing along the marked line.

You can then leave your options open as to which way you want to press the seam allowance when the block is completed.

PREPARATION

Make plastic templates from the patterns provided. Draw around the template on the wrong side of the fabric and cut out the shapes adding a 5mm seam allowance all around.

CUTTING

From the red print, cut four strips 2½in (6.5cm) wide by the length for the outer border. Cut pieces for the blocks as required across the remaining width.

From the green print, cut nine strips 1⅜in (3.5cm) wide across the width for the first border.

From the cream fabric, cut forty-two squares using the 15cm template. Cut twenty-nine squares using the 30cm template. Cut the pieces for the blocks as required from the remainder.

CONSTRUCTION

Make sixty units as in Diagram 1. For each, cut six As in the red print, two As in the green print, four Bs in the cream print, four Cs in the cream print and one 1in (2.5cm) square in the green print. Stitch the As into two sets of four, with the two greens. Join them to complete the star (see Diagram 3).

FINISHED SIZE

- Finished quilt size is 213cm x 254.5cm (84in x 102in).

MATERIALS

- 2.8m (3¼yd) of red print fabric
- 1.6m (1¾yd) of green print fabric
- 30cm (⅓yd) of plain red fabric
- 5m (5½yd) of cream fabric
- 7m (8yd) of backing fabric
- Queen size batting
- Template plastic
- Sharp pencil

STITCHES USED

Running Stitch, Back Stitch

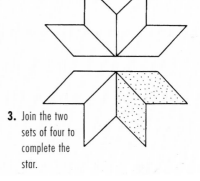

✂ **HELPFUL HINT**

Always place the A template on the fabric in the same way (see Diagram 2). You will automatically have a bias edge next to a straight edge which stops the star 'mushrooming' in the centre.

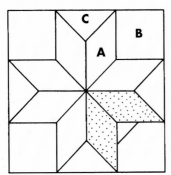

1. The completed star block.

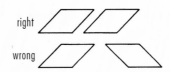

right

wrong

2. Always place the A template on the fabric in the same way, in order to have a bias edge next to a straight edge.

3. Join the two sets of four to complete the star.

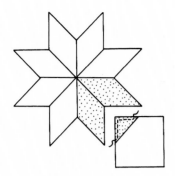

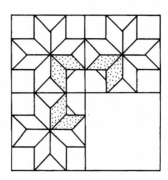

4. Set the cream and green piece into the star between the two green pieces.

5. Join three blocks and a cream 15cm square to form the Double Peony block.

6. Pin and baste the stems in place, tucking the upper raw ends under the pockets.

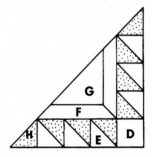

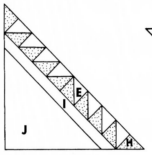

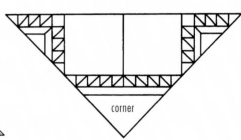

7. Sew three of the E squares in a row with an H piece at one end and stitch this to an F piece.

8. Join the cream and red squares together with an H piece at each end.

9. Stitch two border triangles and a corner piece to each cream pair.

Two sets of four diamonds are joined to complete the star.

Setting the corner piece into the star. This forms a pocket for the stems.

Take the 1in (2.5cm) square of green, fold it in half diagonally and baste it to the corner of one cream B piece.

Set this piece into the star between the two green pieces (see Diagram 4). This forms a pocket in which you can tuck the raw edges of the stems.

Set in the remaining B and C pieces to complete the unit (see Diagram 1).

Join three units and a cream 6in (15cm) square to form the double Peony Block (see Diagram 5).

APPLIQUE

Cut wide strips for the stems and baste the edges under to form a strip of approximately 3in (7.5cm) wide.

Pin and baste the stems in place as in Diagram 6, tucking the upper raw ends under the pockets. Once you have decided on the placement of your stems, it is worth making a placement template to keep the position of the stems consistent for all blocks. Pin and baste the leaves in position.

Appliqué the stems and leaves and then the folded edge of the pocket to enclose the raw ends.

BORDER
TRIANGLES

Make thirty-six triangles as in Diagram 7. For each triangle, cut one of D in the cream fabric, six of E in the cream fabric, six of E in the red print, two of F in the green print, one of G in the plain red and two of H in the red print.

Sew an F piece to either side of the G piece. Sew the cream and red print E pieces into pairs to form squares.

Follow Diagram 7 for the placement of the colours (the shaded part is the red print) and sew three E squares in a row with an H at one end and stitch this to F.

The stems and leaves are appliquéd to the star units to complete the block.

Sew the remaining three E squares together with an H at one end and a D at the other, then sew to the other F piece to complete the triangle.

CORNER PIECES

Make four corner pieces (see Diagram 8). For each corner, cut eight of E in the cream fabric, eight of E in the red print, two of H in the red print, one of I in the green print and one of J in the plain red fabric.

Sew the cream and red E pieces into pairs to form squares.

Follow Diagram 8 for the placement of colour (the red print is shaded). Join these squares together with an H at each end. Stitch this piece to I, and then stitch that to J to complete the corner piece.

ASSEMBLY

Take fourteen of the cream 15cm squares and join them together in pairs. Stitch two border triangles and a corner piece to each pair as in Diagram 9.

Follow the Quilt Layout Diagram to join the blocks, the 11⅞in (30cm) cream squares and the border pieces in diagonal rows. Join the rows together, then add the corner triangles.

BORDERS

Measure the quilt top from the top to the bottom, through the centre to determine the length needed for the first border. Join the 1⅜in (3.5cm) wide strips of green print to the length

Quilt Layout Diagram

Row 1
Row 2
Row 3
Row 4
Row 5
Row 6
Row 7
Row 8
Row 9

required and stitch to the sides of the quilt top.

Measure the quilt top from one side to the other through the centre, join the green strips to this length and stitch to the top and bottom of the quilt top.

Repeat these steps for the outer red border using the 2½in (6.5cm) wide red print strips. Mitre the corners if you prefer.

BACKING

Cut the backing fabric into three equal lengths, remove the selvedges and sew them together to form a piece a little larger than the quilt top.

QUILTING

There are lots of empty spaces free for fancy quilting. A Princess Feather was used as the main design on this quilt. You may prefer to mark the design on the top before basting the layers together, but if you are using stencils or templates, mark them as you go.

BASTING

Layer the backing, batting and quilt top and baste the quilt in a grid with basting lines about 6in to 8in (15cm to 20cm) apart.

FINISHING

BINDING

Bind the quilt edges using the remainder of the red print. This quilt features a single bias binding cut 1¼in (3cm) wide, with folded and mitred corners.

Make a label for the back and sign and date your quilt.

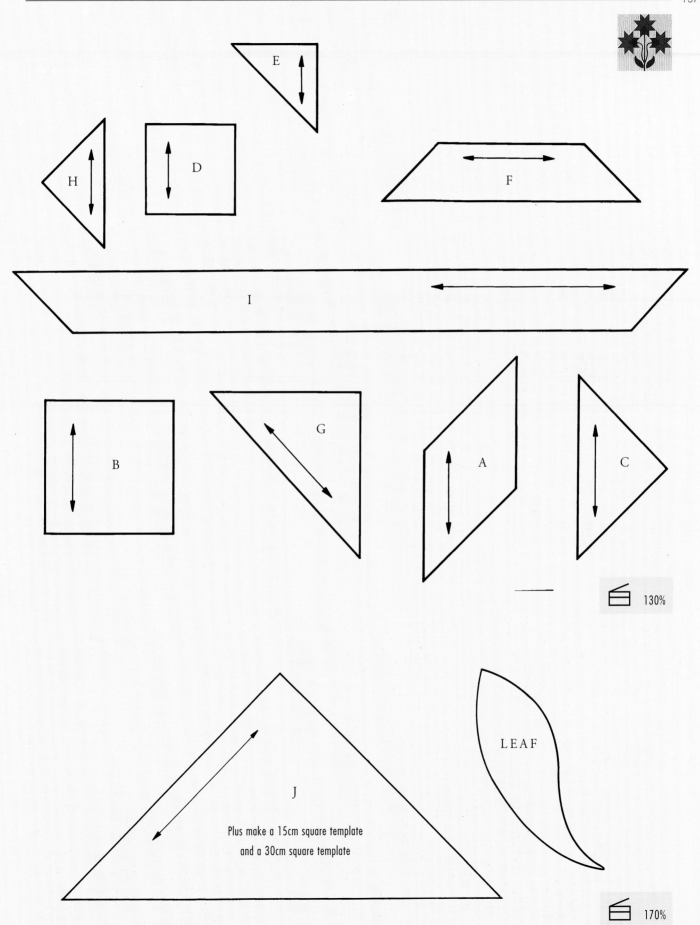

E

H   D   F

I

B   G   A   C

130%

J

Plus make a 15cm square template
and a 30cm square template

LEAF

170%

Antique Sampler Quilt

This breathtaking quilt draws inspiration from the age-old tradition of embroidery samplers. With its quaint pastoral images appliquéd in Herringbone Stitch on osnaburg, it also features Square in a Square blocks with Cross Stitch and appliqué motifs.

BASIC FOUNDATION PIECING

Cut foundations from lightweight tracing paper slightly larger than the finished size and position over the design. Trace the pattern and transfer sewing order numbers. Trim the final block tracing to include ¼in seam allowance. For multiple block designs, try the machine tracing technique. Make a master pattern as above. Stack ten blocks underneath your master. Position the stack underneath the needle of a threadless sewing machine. Sew on the line and machine-trace all the layers at once. Another method of pattern transfer is the photocopier. Due to the inconsistency of some photocopiers, always copy from the same original pattern and make sure your photocopies are the same size. Never copy a photocopy.

LINEN LOOKALIKE

A coarse, even-weave cotton, osnaburg was first manufactured in Osnabrück, Germany. Notable for its use in feed sacks and doll bodies, osnaburg has now been given new life by needleworkers who enjoy quilting and cross stitching on it. Also known as Lin 'n Spun, because of its likeness to linen, osnaburg has a slight slub making it a little heavier than traditional quilting fabrics.

PREPARATION

Trace all the appliqué shapes from the pattern provided onto the dull side of freezer paper. Cut out roughly at least ½in all around the shapes. Iron the

FINISHED SIZE

- Finished quilt size is 175cm x 195.5cm (69in x 77in).

MATERIALS

Fabric requirements are based on 115cm (45in) wide fabrics.

- 4.2m (4½yd) fawn osnaburg
- Large variety of scraps
- 20cm x 15cm (8in x 6in) piece of house fabric
- 2.4m x 6.5cm (94in x 2½in) approx of wide border print
- 1.4m (1½yd) red fabric for scallop border and binding
- 50cm (⅝yd) green fabric for border leaves
- Queen-size cotton/polyester batting
- 4.3m (4¾yd) backing fabric
- Quilter's freezer paper
- Tan stranded embroidery thread
- Size 12 appliqué needles
- Lightweight tracing paper
- Ruler
- Sharp No 2 pencil
- Spray bottle
- Tweezers
- Mediumweight cardboard

STITCHES USED

Buttonhole Stitch, Herringbone Stitch

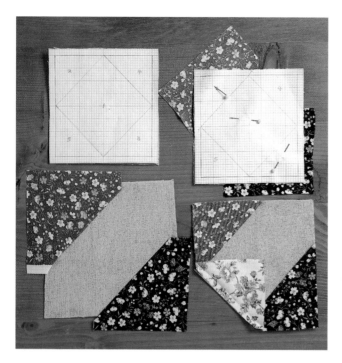

Pieces positioned on the osnaburg square to construct the Square in a Square block.

The completed Square in a Square block with Broderie Perse motif ready to stitch in place.

shiny side of the paper onto the wrong side of the chosen fabrics.

Cut out on the pencil line, through both the fabric and the paper. This gives a nice sharp edge to your appliqué piece. There is no turning under.

CONSTRUCTION

APPLIQUE

Cut a 17in square of osnaburg. Peel paper off the appliqué pieces and place it onto the background fabric using the photograph as a guide. Aim to keep them within a 15in square. Baste into position.

Using one strand of embroidery thread, buttonhole or herringbone stitch loosely round the shapes (see the Stitch Diagrams on pages 158–161). Any pieces likely to fray are best left on the freezer paper until you have time to stitch them properly. Remember, you are not turning

under any seam allowances.

The reindeer antlers are worked in Stem Stitch. Trim the finished appliqué piece to 16½in square.

FIRST BORDER

Think carefully about the border print you plan to use. In this quilt, the border print has uniformly-spaced rosettes which allow for a nice, even effect at the mitred corners.

Firstly, find the centre point of each of the four sides of the appliqué piece. Mark with a pin. Take your chosen border print and find a design within it that can be positioned at the centre points. Mark it with a pin. Cut a strip 2½in x 23in, keeping the pin in the centre. Cut three more identical strips and mark the centres with pins.

Measure out from the pins one half the size of the side measurement of the appliqué piece and pin on the border print. Repeat for the other end. Mark all four border strips this way.

Lay a border strip on the opposite

sides of the appliqué piece, right sides together, matching the pins at centre points and ends. Sew the border strips in place, beginning and ending ¼in from each corner. Do not cut off excess fabric. Fold back all four ends and press at a 45 degree angle.

Take the remaining two border strips and repeat steps as before. The second set of border strips must extend under the folded corners of the previously sewn border strips.

To mitre the corners, pin the ends of the border strips along the fold lines, sew together and press.

SQUARE WITHIN A SQUARE BLOCK

The main body of the quilt is made up of two hundred and thirty Square in a Square blocks, each measuring 4in finished. If you use the Foundation Block Template provided on the Pattern Sheet, you will be able to keep the blocks uniform, making it easier to match seam lines when the blocks are assembled.

Photocopy the pattern or draw up your own foundation sheets on graph paper.

From the length of the osnaburg, cut the four outside scalloped border strips, 4¾in x 70in. These will be adjusted later.

From the remainder, cut 4½in strips across the width of the fabric and cross cut into two hundred and thirty 4½in squares. These will be used for position No 1 on the foundation. Use your scrap pieces for the corners, making sure they are big enough to cover the seam allowances.

Begin with fabric No 1, right side up, over position No 1 on the foundation back. Hold it up to the light to see that the fabric extends beyond the seam allowance. Use a glue stick or pin to position No 1.

Place a scrap right side down on top of No 1. Flip the entire unit over while holding the fabrics and foundation with your thumb and forefinger. Position the sewing machine needle about ¼in outside the sewing line joining fabric units No 1 and No 2.

Lower the needle and sew on the line, through the foundation and fabrics, to several stitches past the line. Raise the needle and cut the thread.

Open fabric No 2 and check that it covers position No 2 on the foundation.

Fold back the fabrics and pattern and trim the seam to ¼in. Open and finger-press or use a dry iron.

Add the remaining shapes in numerical order. See step-by-step photographs for the foundation technique.

Make two hundred and thirty blocks. Trim each block to exactly 4½in square.

If you plan to cross stitch or appliqué a motif in each block, carefully remove the papers now. If not, leave them in until the quilt top is completed.

BLOCK EMBELLISHMENT

Each block has its own individual motif. Patterns are not provided for these.

However, you can cut the designs from novelty fabrics or cross stitch motifs onto the osnaburg. As with the centre appliqué, images are stitched in place, using herringbone or buttonhole stitch.

Ideas for embellishment include animals, birds, houses, jugs, flowers and patchwork blocks.

ASSEMBLY

Sew five blocks together in a row, taking care to match all points. Press the seam allowances to one side. Make ten of these rows.

Sew five rows together, making sure that the seam allowances notch into each other. Press with the row seam allowances all facing down. Sew this section to the left side of the quilt top and press again.

Sew another five rows of blocks together as before. Stitch this section to the right side of the quilt top.

Sew fifteen blocks together in a row and press. Make twelve of these rows.

Sew six of the rows together and press. Sew this unit to the top of the quilt, taking care to match seam allowances. Press the seams down.

Sew another six rows of blocks together. Sew this section to the bottom of the quilt top and press the seam allowances down.

Remove the paper foundations. A spray bottle of water will help for stubborn pieces, as will tweezers.

SCALLOP BORDER

Draw the scallop by tracing the cardboard shape provided. For the side borders, you will need two strips of osnaburg measuring 4¾in x 68½in and four strips of red fabric measuring 1½in x 68½in. You will need to join the red strips together to make up the 68½in length. Place the cardboard template onto the scallop border fabric and draw pencil lines around the shape (see Diagram 1).

Place one strip of scallop material on top of an osnaburg strip, right sides facing up. Pin these together. Machine sew ¼in from the inner raw edges of the border. This is Row A. Machine sew ¼in from the outer side of the scallop strip, using a slightly longer stitch. This is Row B.

Row A stitching line remains and is sewn to the blocks. Row B is removed scallop by scallop (see Diagram 2).

With sharp scissors, undo 3in of the Row B stitching. Cut on the drawn scallop lines, making sure to cut right into the indentation between the scallops. There will be no turning under of the seam allowances.

Using a herringbone or buttonhole stitch, appliqué the scallops to the osnaburg, taking a couple of extra stitches at the bottom of the scallop to prevent fraying. Continue in this way, undoing Row B and appliquéing each scallop, until one side of the border is complete.

Repeat these steps for the outer edge of the border, making sure the scallops are a mirror image of the opposite side.

Make a second side border the same.

Pin borders to either side of the quilt top, taking care to match the bottoms of the scallops to the seam lines and centre points of the blocks. Machine stitch borders to the quilt, stitching slightly over the Row A seam line. Press and trim.

For the top and bottom borders, use two strips of osnaburg 4¾in x 69in and four strips of red fabric 1½in x 69in.

Repeat steps as before. When you get to the outside border, you will need to appliqué a separate corner scallop piece at each corner one additional scallop to extend the ends of the side borders.

Using the leaf template, cut one hundred and thirty-two leaves and arrange them evenly between the rows of scallops. Buttonhole or herringbone stitch the leaves in position as shown in the photograph.

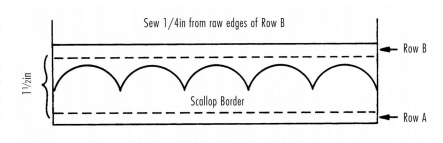

Diagram 1
Place cardboard scallop template onto fabric and trace around.

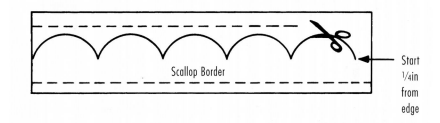

Digram 2
Cut on the drawn scallop lines, making sure to cut right into the indentation between the scallops.

QUILTING

Cut the backing material in half and sew together lengthwise, removing the selvedges.

Layer backing, batting and quilt top and baste securely. Quilt as desired.

FINISHING

BINDING

You will need approx 8m (8¾yd) of straight-edge double binding. Cut seven 2½in strips across the width of the fabric and join diagonally. Press in half lengthwise. Align raw edge of binding with raw edge of quilt top and sew together, using ¼in seam allowance and mitring corners. Fold to the back and slip stitch in place.

Make a label and attach it to the back. Sign and date your quilt.

125%

BORDER LEAF

Dresden Plate

This Prairie Flower variation of the popular Dresden Plate Block is reminiscent of bygone days and lends itself nicely to old-fashioned prints. This pattern involves both machine piecing and hand appliqué.

PREPARATION

Using cardboard or template plastic, make a template from the petal template design provided. The seam allowance has been included in the template.

Using the template, cut out two hundred and sixteen plate wedges from assorted fabrics.

CONSTRUCTION

PIECING

With the right sides together, fold the Dresden wedge in half lengthwise and stitch across the edge (see Diagram 1). Trim the seam, turn the wedge right side out and press it flat with the seam at the back (similar to the end of a tie).

Lay twelve different wedges out as you would like them to appear. Sew the wedges into pairs, then sew the pairs together to make quarters of the Dresden Plate (see Diagram 2).

Join the quarters to make halves, then stitch the halves together to complete the plate.

Make eighteen of these plates and press them carefully (see Diagram 3). Cut the cream background fabric into a piece, 78½in x 48½in. Fold this piece in half, then in half again, creasing lightly. Unfold the fabric, fold it in half, then in half again in the other direction, creasing lightly.

Using the creases as guidelines, position the Dresden Plates on the background fabric following the Layout Diagram provided. Pin, or baste them in place. Appliqué the eighteen plates using

Fold the petals, stitch across the end, trim, turn out and press to form the points at the end of the petals.

a blind hem stitch (see Diagram 4).

Make a cardboard or plastic template from the centre circle template pattern provided. Trace the template eighteen times onto lightweight cardboard (gift cards are ideal) and cut out accurately. Cut out the centre fabrics using the cardboard cut-outs as a guide and adding ¼in seam allowance.

Use a small gathering stitch close to the outer raw edge to draw the fabric around the paper. Anchor the thread and press the circle. Remove the card and appliqué the circle over the centre of the Dresden Plate.

PIECED BORDER

For the pieced border, cut forty-two rectangles 6½in x 3½in from an assortment of fabrics. Cut one hundred and sixty-eight 2in squares from the quilters' muslin. Draw a diagonal line from corner to corner on the wrong side of the cream squares.

FINISHED SIZE

- Finished size is 210cm x 135cm (84in x 54in).

MATERIALS

- Assorted scraps, a total of 3.6m x 1.15m (4⅛yd x 1⅓yd) is needed for the petals, centres and outer border

- 2.5m x (2½yd) of 150mm wide quilters' muslin for background, borders and binding

- 4.4m (5yd) backing fabric

- 2.3m x 1.5m (2⅔yd x 1⅔yd) batting

- Neutral thread

- Appliqué and quilting needle

- Cardboard or template plastic for templates

- Sewing machine and general sewing supplies

NOTE: Pre-wash all fabrics before using. ¼in (6mm) seam allowance is used throughout.

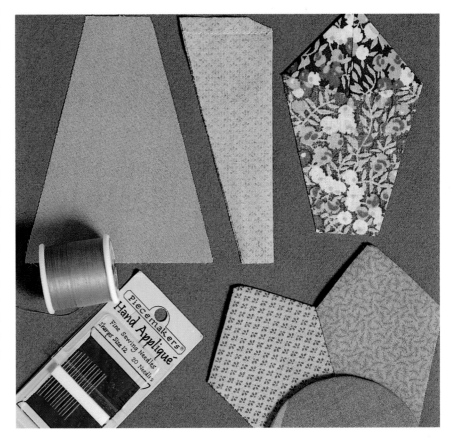

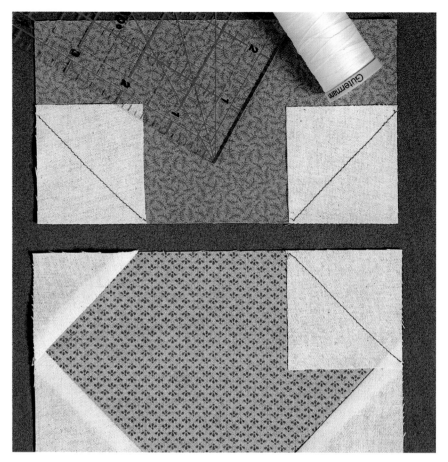

Place the background squares on each end of one long side of the rectangle with right sides together and sew along the drawn line. Trim the corner of the triangle, leaving the seam allowance (see Diagram 5).

Press the first two squares to the back and similarly add squares to the remaining two corners of the rectangle (see Diagram 6).

Cut four 3½in squares from the blue scraps for the corner squares. Make two rows of thirteen pieced rectangles joined end to end. Join these rows to the sides of the quilt top.

Make two rows of eight pieced rectangles and add a blue corner square to each end of both rows. Make two of these rows, sew a corner square to both ends then sew the rows to the top and bottom of the quilt. Press.

Join 2in squares to each corner of the border rectangles.

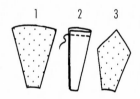

1. With right sides together, fold the petal in half lengthwise and stitch across the edge.

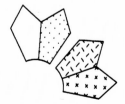

2. Sew the petals together in pairs and then sew the pairs together to make quarters of the Dresden Plate.

3. Join the quarters to make halves, then stitch the halves together to complete the Plate.

4. Appliqué the 18 Plates onto the background using a blind hem stitch.

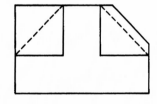

5. Place 2in squares onto two corners of the rectangle with right sides together and sew along the drawn diagonal lines.

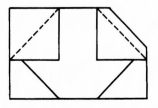

6. Join squares onto the remaining two corners of the rectangle.

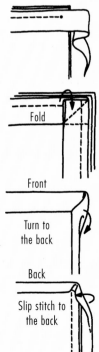

7. Follow the steps to accurately mitre the binding.

QUILTING

Layer the backing, batting and quilt top and baste or pin it together. Hand-quilt in the ditch between each petal and around each plate, then hand stipple-quilt over the background.

FINISHING

BINDING

Cut and join 2½in strips of the quilters' muslin to make a continuous length to go around all sides of the quilt. Press the binding in half lengthwise with the wrong sides together. Trim the backing and batting to be even with the quilt top on all sides.

Pin the folded binding to the top of the quilt, matching the raw edges. Sew through the binding and all layers of the quilt by machine leaving ¼in seam allowance from the edge of the quilt, mitring the corners as you go and following the steps in Diagram 7.

Turn the binding to the back of the quilt and slip stitch firmly in place.

Make a label and attach it to the back. Sign and date your quilt.

Fold lines

Centre

LAYOUT DIAGRAM

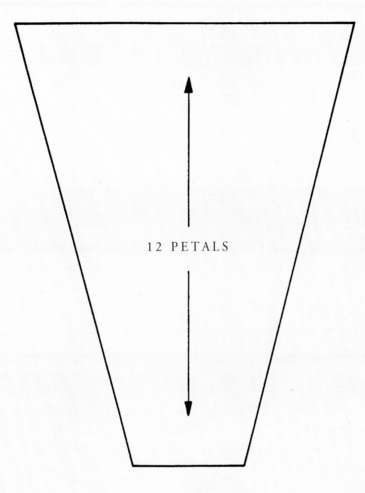

12 PETALS

PETAL TEMPLATE

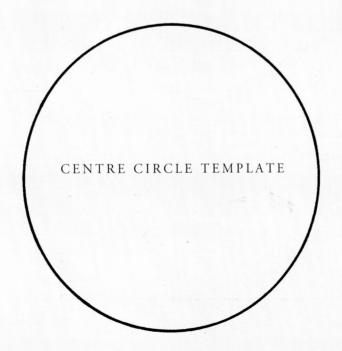

CENTRE CIRCLE TEMPLATE

SS

Fragrant Florals

*In this traditional quilt, country flowers frame a
basket of blossoms. The appliquéd centre medallion is surrounded
by a quilted tone-on-tone background and the traditional
pieced border showcases a myriad of floral fabrics.*

PREPARATION

All pieced sections are cut with a rotary cutter and quilter's ruler.

All measurements for this quilt include ¼in seam allowance.

NOTE: Read all the instructions carefully before beginning the quilt. Cut all the requirements for the pieced borders first and then use the remaining pieces for the appliqué.

CUTTING

Refer to the cutting guide diagram to get the best use of the fabric:

From the beige background, cut one 17¾in square centre-applique block. Cut two 16in squares. Cut these in half diagonally to make a total of four half-square triangles.

Cut four 6½in x 52in strips for the Sawtooth Border background.

From the fabric for the Chocolate Borders, cut fourteen 2½in strips across the width of the fabric. Two will be used for the border around the centre block, four for the Chocolate Border (Part 1) and eight for the Chocolate Border (Part 2).

For the first Pieced Border of 3in blocks, cut the following:

From the tan background, cut two 4½in x 45in strips. Cross cut these to make twenty 4½in squares. Cut these across the diagonal twice to make eighty triangles.

Cut four 3½in squares and set these aside for the corner blocks.

From each of the three pink fabrics, cut one 4¼in x 45in strip. From these three strips, cut three squares from two fabrics and four from the third, a total of ten 4¼in squares. Cut across the diagonal twice to make forty triangles.

From one pink fabric, cut four 2½in squares for the centre border corners.

From each of the five blue fabrics, cut one 4¼in x 45in strip. From these five strips, cut a total of ten squares (two from each colour). Cut as above to make forty triangles.

From the length of the fabric for the Sawtooth Borders cut, eight strips, 1½ in wide.

From the fabric for the Mustard Border, cut eight 1½in strips.

For the second Pieced Border of 5in blocks at the top and bottom of the quilt, from the assorted beige and blue fabrics cut a total of ten, 6¼in squares. Cut each square twice across the diagonal to yield 80 squares.

From the fabric for the floral Outer Border, cut eight 6½in strips across the width of the fabric.

From the fabric for the binding, cut eight 2½in strips across the width of the fabric.

CONSTRUCTION

APPLIQUE

Using the design provided, trace the outline onto the 17¾in background centre square, and set on point.

Choose fabrics for the flowers and leaves. Appliqué in the method you prefer. Freezer paper has been used here to eliminate the need for template making. Iron it onto the back of the fabric.

Complete the basket appliqué first, then embroider the flowers.

Using one strand of embroidery cotton for the flower centres, use pistil stitch and French knots (see Stitch Guide pages 158–161). Use two strands for the lavender, a combination of light and dark shades of mauve, and stitch using bullion stitch.

FINISHED SIZE

• Finished quilt size is 168cm x 203cm (66in x 80in).

MATERIALS

NOTE: Fabric lengths are based on a standard width of 115cm (45in)

• 1.5m (1¾yd) beige background fabric
• 1.4m (1⅔yd) fabric for the Sawtooth Border

FIRST PIECED BORDER

• 45cm (½yd) tan background fabric
• 15cm (¼yd) each of three pink fabrics
• 15cm (¼yd) each of five blue fabrics
• 45cm (½yd) fabric for the Mustard Border
• 1m (1⅛yd) fabric for the Chocolate Borders

SECOND PIECED BORDER

• 20cm (¼yd) each of four blue fabrics
• 20cm (¼yd) each of four beige fabrics
• 1.6m (1¾yd) Floral Outer Border

APPLIQUE

• 30cm (⅓yd) green fabric
• Assorted fabric pieces for appliquéd flowers and leaves
• 30cm (⅓yd) fabric for basket
• 65cm (¾yd) fabric for binding
• 3.6m (4yd) backing fabric
• Batting to fit
• Threads to match appliqué
• White fabric pencil
• Freezer paper
• Machine or hand-quilting cotton
• Embroidery cottons
• Rotary cutter, ruler and mat

STITCHES USED

Appliqué Stitch, Bullion Stitch, French Knots, Pistil Stitch

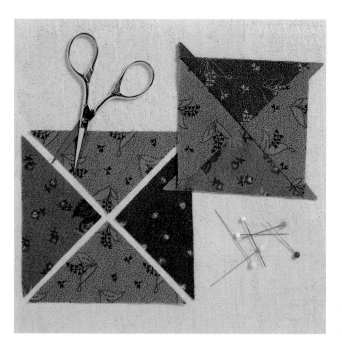

Cutting and positioning the block for the Pieced Border.

The Sawtooth Border. Mark seamline and cutting lines.
Cut and fold ready to stitch.

BORDERS

Centre Border

Using one of the 2½in strips cut for the Chocolate Border, cut into two 17¾in strips. Attach these strips to the opposite sides of the centre block.

Measure and cut the other strip into two 17¾in strips and attach the 2½in pink squares to each end. Sew to the remaining sides of the centre.

Set the medallion block on point by attaching the large background triangles.

First Pieced Border

After completing all the cutting for this border, you will have one hundred and sixty triangles. Decide on the colour combinations for the blocks. Sew one tan triangle to one blue or one pink triangle. This will produce eighty larger triangles.

Sew together a combination of tan and blue, matched with tan and pink, to make a square. This will produce forty squares.

Sew ten squares together for each side border (see Diagram 2).

Attach a 10-square first border to either side of the centre square. Attach the 3½in tan squares (previously set aside) to each end of the remaining two borders, then sew these to the top and bottom of the centre square.

Sawtooth Border

Using the 1½in strips cut from the Sawtooth Border fabric, on the reverse side of the fabric, rule a line the length of the strip, 1in from one side with the white fabric pencil (see step-by-step photograph and Diagram 3). From that line, mark a 1in cutting line to the other side at 2in intervals and mark the mid-point of each segment to indicate the point, prior to folding. Cut on the cutting lines and fold back the sections to create a sawtooth effect. Press the sawtooth border with a hot iron.

Find the centre of the 6½in strips for the background to the Sawtooth Border. Position the inner sawtooth strip in place, starting in the centre with nine points on either side. Appliqué the points into position.

Position the outer sawtooth as above, with twelve points on either side of the centre. Attach the Sawtooth Borders to the quilt, mitring the corners.

Appliqué on Sawtooth Border

From the green fabric for the appliqué, cut eight 1¼in x 16in bias stems. Press them in half with wrong sides together. Using the pattern as a guide, position these at the four corners.

Mustard Border

Measure carefully through the centre of the quilt to determine the length. Cut the side border strips to length and attach, making sure the join is centred. At this stage, the quilt should measure 50½in square.

Measure the quilt top widthwise, cut and attach the top and bottom borders, centring the join.

Chocolate Border (Part 1)

Join the 2½in strips cut for the first part of the Chocolate Border to fit the width of the quilt and attach it to the top and bottom.

Second Pieced Border

Arrange the 80 triangles cut from the beige and blue fabrics into a pleasing colour combination and join in the same manner as the first pieced border.

Sew two rows of ten blocks each and attach these to the top and bottom of the quilt centre.

Chocolate Border (Part 2)

Join the eight remaining 2½in strips cut for the border, to fit the top and bottom of the quilt. Centre the join and attach these strips. Measure the length of the quilt, join the strips to fit and attach to the sides, again centring the join.

Final Outer Border

Measure the quilt across the width. It should be approximately 54½in wide. Join the strips cut for the floral borders to fit this measurement and attach them to the top and bottom. Measure the length of the quilt through the centre. It should be approximately 80in. Join the remaining strips to fit this length and attach to the sides of the quilt.

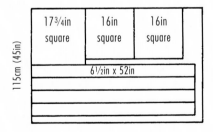

1. Cutting diagram for beige background fabric

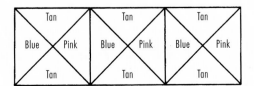

2. Sew the triangles together in colour sequence.

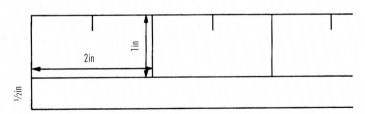

3. Mark the measurements for the sawtooth border.

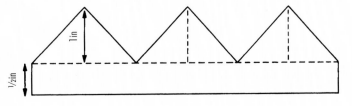

QUILTING

❖

Sandwich the backing, cotton batting and the quilt top together. Baste or pin the layers in place. Quilt by hand or a machine in ³⁄₄in squares behind the appliqué centre, and then in 1in lines in the corner diamonds around the centre. Quilting on the Sawtooth Border is worked in 1½in lines at an angle of 45 degrees from point to point. The floral border is quilted in 1in lines at right angles to the quilt centre, leaving the corners unquilted. The blocks in the pieced borders are quilted in the ditch.

FINISHING

❖

Cut the backing fabric in half. Remove selvedges and sew together lengthwise.

BINDING

Using the strips cut for the binding, join them end to end, into one long length. Press in half with wrong sides together. With raw edges together, stitch the binding strip to the front of the quilt, folding the corners into mitres as you go. Turn the binding to the back of the quilt and slip stitch it into place.

Make a label for the back and sign and date your quilt.

FRAGRANT FLORALS QUILT
CONSTRUCTION DIAGRAM

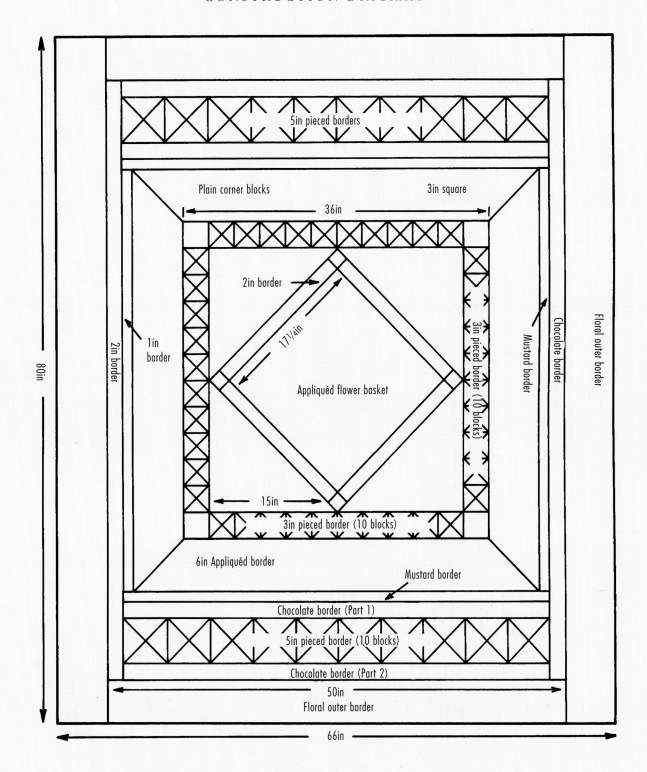

5in pieced borders

Plain corner blocks

3in square

36in

2in border

3in square

3in pieced border (10 blocks)

17¼in

Mustard border

Chocolate border

Floral outer border

Appliquéd flower basket

2in border

1in border

2in border

15in

3in pieced border (10 blocks)

6in Appliquéd border

Mustard border

Chocolate border (Part 1)

5in pieced border (10 blocks)

Chocolate border (Part 2)

80in

50in

Floral outer border

66in

Stitch Guide

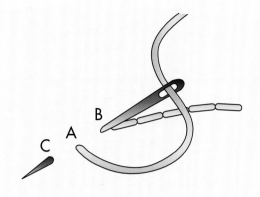

BACK STITCH

❖

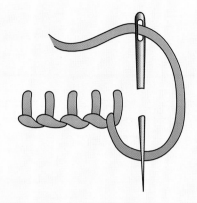

BLANKET STITCH

❖

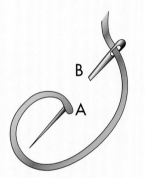 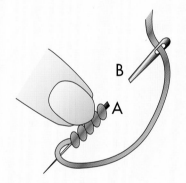 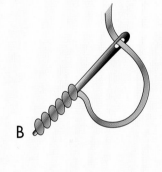

BULLION STITCH

❖

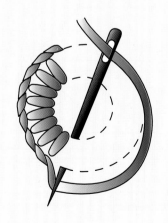

BUTTONHOLE STITCH

❖

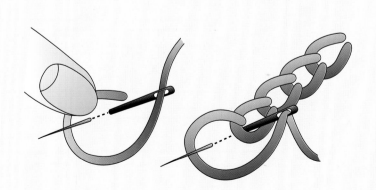

CHAIN STITCH

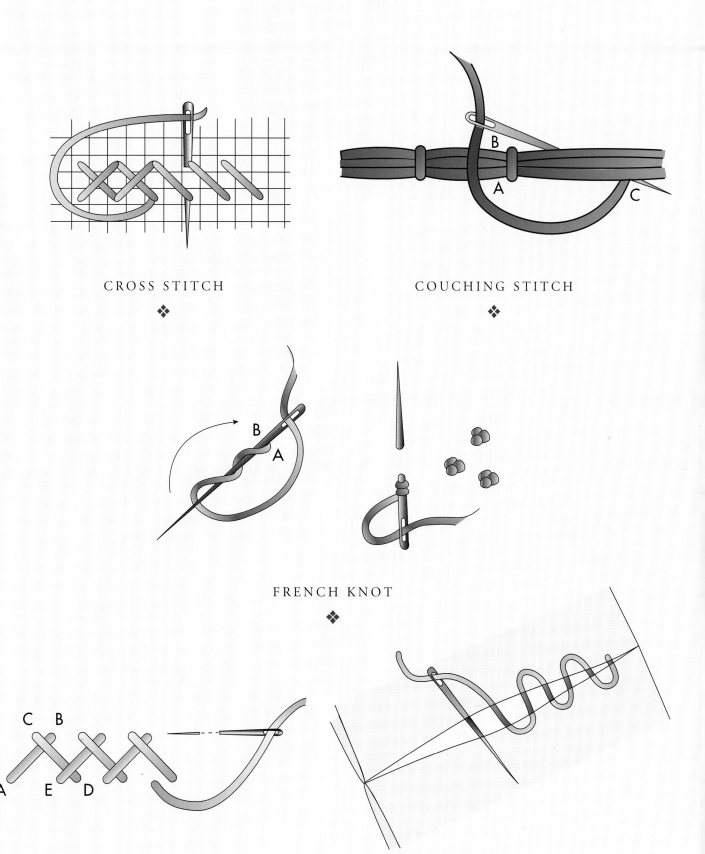

CROSS STITCH

COUCHING STITCH

FRENCH KNOT

HERRINGBONE STITCH

LADDER STITCH

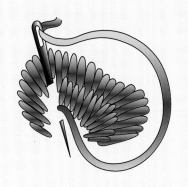

LONG AND SHORT STITCH

❖

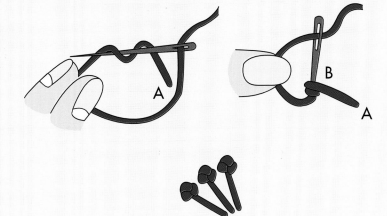

PISTIL STITCH

❖

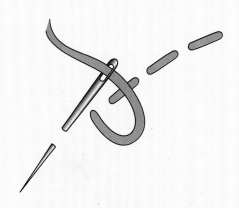

RUNNING STITCH

❖

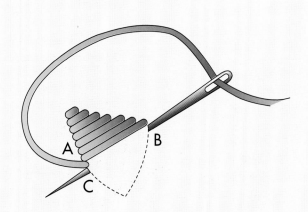

SATIN STITCH

❖

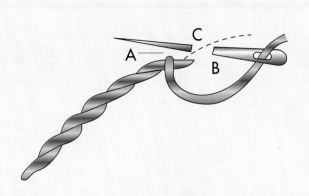

STEM STITCH: THREAD DOWN

❖

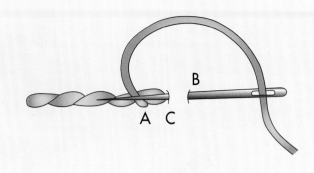

STEM STITCH: THREAD UP

❖

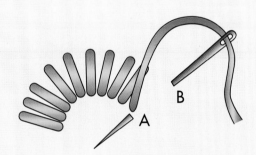

STRAIGHT STITCH

❖

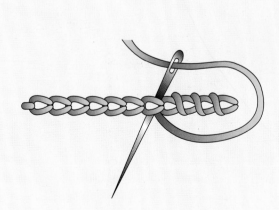

WHIPPED CHAIN STITCH

❖

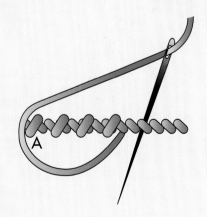

WHIPPED STEM STITCH

❖

Basic Equipment

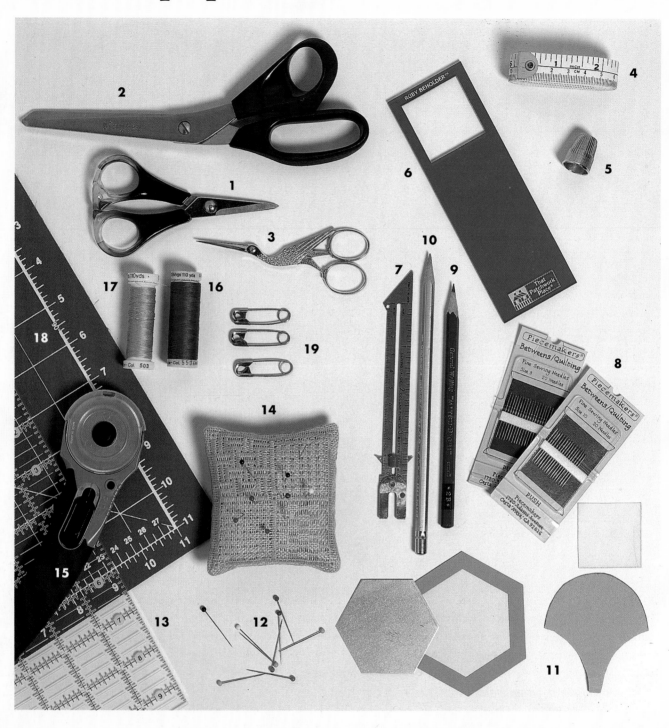

KEY

1	Paper Cutting Scissors	**8**	Needles	**15**	Rotary Cutter
2	Dressmakers' Scissors	**9**	HB Pencil	**16**	100% Cotton Thread
3	Embroidery Scissors	**10**	Silver Marking Pencil	**17**	Cotton/Polyester Thread
4	Tape Measure	**11**	Templates	**18**	Cutting Mat
5	Thimble	**12**	Glass Headed Pins	**19**	Safety Pins
6	Ruby Beholder	**13**	Plastic Ruler		
7	Adjustable Ruler	**14**	Pin Cushion		

BASIC EQUIPMENT

We may have come a long way since appliqué quilts were first made in the 1880s, but the basic tools for appliqué such as needles, thread, pins and scissors remain the essentials.

NEEDLES

For machine stitching you will need a supply of new sewing machine needles for light to medium-weight cottons.

A 'betweens' needle is considered the best for both hand piecing and quilting. 'Sharps' are used when a longer needle is required. A good general rule is to use as fine a needle as you can manage comfortably; size 8 is recommended for beginners. If you want to make smaller stitches as you progress, use a smaller needle. Size 12 is the smallest.

THREAD

Traditionally, synthetic threads are used with synthetic fabrics and cotton with cotton fabrics. Polyester-cotton thread (polyester core wrapped in cotton) or 100 per cent cotton thread are best for cotton fabrics and are the easiest to use for all other fabrics. This thread does have a tendency to fray and tangle so avoid this by knotting the end before unrolling the thread, then cutting and threading the other end through the needle.

Select a colour that matches the darkest fabric you are sewing. If you are using different fabrics, select a neutral thread such as grey or ecru which will blend inconspicuously with all of them.

PINS

Glass headed pins are very sharp and good for piercing straight through the material when lining up a seam or a starting point.

There are longer pins available which are excellent for pinning together layers on more bulky projects.

SCISSORS

You will need three pairs of scissors for appliqué. Dressmakers' shears, preferably with a bent handle – these should be extremely sharp and used only for cutting fabric. Paper scissors – never cut paper with sewing shears, as this will dull the blades. Embroidery scissors for clipping threads and seam allowances – these should also be very sharp.

ROTARY CUTTER AND MAT

A rotary cutter is an excellent tool for cutting strips, straightening fabric edges and cutting out a variety of geometric patchwork pieces. It also enables more accurate cutting of several layers of fabric at once.

Choose a cutter with a large blade, and keep spare blades handy. Always cut on a mat specially designed for a rotary cutter to keep the blade sharp. Fold the fabric in half on the mat with right sides facing and selvedges matching. The drafting triangle sits directly on the fold of the fabric, the rotary rule sits on the left edge of the triangle. The mat grips the fabric and helps the blade to cut straight. A 'self-healing' cutting mat is ideal.

RULERS

A long, clear plastic ruler is a must to use with a rotary cutter. These rulers are well marked and sturdy and there is no danger of shaving off a piece of the ruler when cutting layers of fabric.

PENCILS

A soft lead pencil is the traditional option for marking a design, but there is also a variety of marking pencils available. Probably the most useful is a water soluble pencil, as it gradually fades after a period of time.

Be careful, however, as the design is liable to disappear before the project can be finished.

TEMPLATES

Templates can be homemade from graph paper, tracing paper and cardboard or template plastic. The edges of cardboard templates tend to wear after frequent cutting of patches, but plastic and metal templates, which are available in a great variety of shapes and sizes, are virtually indestructible. This is a great advantage, especially for a large project which requires cutting out several of each shape.

Window templates are useful if you are featuring or centring a motif or flower in a patch.

Templates for hand sewing, appliqué and quilting are cut to the exact shape without seam allowance. They mark the stitching line not the cutting line. For machine sewing, include a ¼in (6mm) seam allowance around all edges.

THIMBLES

A thimble is indispensable if you are quilting by hand. It is also good to use on the finger underneath the work to push the needle back through the fabric.

FRAMES AND HOOPS

A frame or a hoop makes the quilting of large projects, such as bed-sized quilts, much easier. It is not essential to use one for smaller items, but you will get a better finish.

FABRICS

Choosing the most suitable fabric for your appliqué project is important, especially for a beginner. Some fabrics are easier to work with than others. With experience, you will discover which fabric is a joy to use and which is an absolute headache. The most important rules to remember are to buy the best fabric you can afford. A firmly woven, lightweight, 100 per cent pure cotton, which is easier to use, lasts longer and gives crisp results.

Synthetics and mixtures can be difficult to iron and handle and may pucker along the seams but they are attractive, versatile and can be unusual or striking in appearance. They are often more readily available than 100 per cent cottons, but they are not all easier to use. Some tend to be slippery, floppy and soft.

As you gain experience, you may want to experiment with more exotic fabrics. Many of these will need special handling but to find out about these fabrics, you will have to test them yourself. Some satins and taffeta can be too fragile for

appliqué. Synthetics also tend to be more difficult to quilt through as they are slightly spongy.

COLOURS AND PRINTS

The successful combining of colours is often a matter of trial and error, not something that can be taught. The only way to find out if it will work is by trying it.

To achieve a good contrast, you need a mix of prints: small, medium, large, checks, stripes and plains. A mix of colours is also important. Contrast rather than coordinate. You will need a mixture of colour values – twenty per cent darks, forty per cent mediums and forty per cent lights is a good mix.

The value, or the lightness or darkness of a colour is probably more important than the actual colour when you are making a quilt. To achieve successful results, try to use a range of values.

Many small-scale floral prints are available. Although a safe choice, they are sometimes so safe and well colour-coordinated that they give a rather dull and uninspired finished effect.

Experiment with prints of varying scale, stripes and border designs, geometric prints and checks. Some large-scale prints can introduce a delicate, lacy effect. Take particular care with stripes. If they are not cut and sewn perfectly straight, it will be very obvious.

Certain fabrics are evocative of different eras or styles. Create a country-style quilt by including fabrics which are bold and brightly coloured and include different-sized checks, stripes, ticking, stars and geometric prints.

A 1930s style quilt can be created by including fabrics such as bright pastels, fresh florals, perky checks, stripes and white backgrounds.

FABRICS TO AVOID

Stretch fabrics such as knits and some crepes should always be avoided. Very closely woven fabrics can also prove difficult, even for machine sewing. This applies to heavy fabrics such as canvas, and lightweight fabrics like some poplins.

Very open weave fabrics can cause difficulties as they tend to fray and be transparent.

PREPARATION OF FABRICS

Always wash your fabrics before use. This will pre-shrink them, remove excess dye and remove any sizing, so that the fabric is easier to handle. Machine wash your fabrics unless you have only a small quantity of fabric.

The volume of water used for washing seems to flush the dye and sizing out thoroughly. It is unusual to have a problem such as the dye running from one fabric to others, but if you are not sure of a fabric, always hand wash it separately.

If tumble drying, a short drying time is quite sufficient, unless the pieces are very large.

Don't over-dry fabrics, as they may become very creased. Remove while they are still slightly damp, then iron them.

When you are purchasing batting for your quilt, it is important to read the washing instructions before you make your choice. Some synthetic battings are often unsuitable for ordinary laundering. Always choose natural fibre battings such as wool, cotton or silk. A good mixture is 90 per cent cotton and 10 per cent polyester. This blend is suitable for both hand and machine quilting and it also washes very well.

Conversion Chart for Fabrics

In that cupboard full of treasured fabrics that every dedicated quilter owns, there are special favourites that are only 90cm wide, when you need 115cm or 150cm width for a special project. Our chart below will show you how to convert the fabric to the width you need.

WIDTH	90cm	115cm	150cm
MEASUREMENT	1.6m	1.3m	0.9m
	1.8m	1.5m	1.1m
	2.1m	1.6m	1.3m
	2.3m	1.9m	1.5m
	2.6m	2.1m	1.6m
	2.9m	2.3m	1.7m
	3.1m	2.5m	1.8m
	3.4m	2.6m	2.1m
	3.9m	2.9m	2.2m
	4.1m	3.1m	2.4m
	4.3m	3.3m	2.5m
	4.6m	3.5m	2.6m

If one of your favourite fabrics is 90cm wide and the size you require is 2.5m x 115cm, go down to the 2.5m in the 115cm column and directly across to the 90cm column. You will need 3.1m of the 90cm fabric for the same project. Remember to allow a little more for napped fabric.

Basic Instructions

Appliqué quilts can be made in many different ways. Here we give you the basic techniques required to successfully complete a quilt.

DESIGN AND DRAFTING

❖

To adapt a design or border, or see how the quilt will look and fit together, you will need to make a sketch on graph paper.

Graph paper is used for two things – to make small sketches of quilt designs (graph plan) and to make full size drawings of shapes for templates or as guides for rotary cutting.

You can play with different colourings with a graph plan and use it as a reference map as you construct your quilt. This helps to see the relative proportions of the border and quilt and to judge the effect. A sketch also lets you preview your quilt and make improvements before you start cutting and sewing.

A quilt sketch is a drawing of the quilt in miniature. You will need to assign a scale in order to calculate the finished size of the quilt and to draft templates. Keep the scale easy so that cutting dimensions will match standard markings on your rotary cutting ruler.

DRAFTING TEMPLATES

❖

Graph paper marked in ¼in is one of the easiest to use to make full size drawings of template shapes. You can draw a full-size block or portion of a border onto graph paper and identify each shape to be cut by lightly colouring it in, then add a consistent ¼in seam allowance around each one. Trace the completed shapes onto template material or use the

measurements as cutting guides for template-free rotary cutting.

Template plastic with a ¼in grid is also available, so that shapes can be drawn directly onto it and an accurate seam allowance added. If the templates are to be used for machine sewing, add a ¼in seam allowance all around. If the template is being used for hand sewing, add a ¼in seam allowance when cutting out the fabric. Straight grain arrows should be marked onto templates.

NOTE: The outside edges of a block or quilt must always be on the straight grain, or the quilt will not lie flat. Mark your graphed blocks and borders accordingly.

Gluing a piece of sandpaper to the back of a paper or plastic template, with the gritty side facing down, is a great way of cutting accurate shapes from fabric.

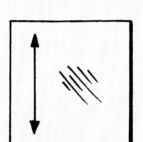

Standard Template

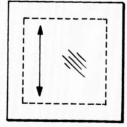

Machine Sewing Template

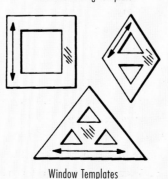

Window Templates

The sandpaper adds weight and sturdiness and the rough surface grips the fabric for more accurate cutting.

NOTE: Do not cut your sandpaper with fabric scissors.

CUTTING

Trim the selvedge from the fabric before you begin. If you are using one fabric for both borders and block pieces, cut the borders first, then the block pieces from what is left over.

Position the templates on the fabric so that the arrows match the straight grain of the fabric. With a sharp pencil (an erasable pencil or a white for dark fabrics, or lead pencil for light fabrics), trace around the template on the fabric. Allow a further ¼in all around the drawn shape for seam allowance before cutting out. Templates for machine sewing usually include a seam allowance, but these pieces must be precisely cut as there is no drawn line to guide your sewing. Multiple layers can be cut at the one time by folding and pressing the fabric into layers before placing the template. Make sure that each piece is cut on the straight grain.

ROTARY OR TEMPLATE-FREE CUTTING

❖

It is important to use the rotary cutter accurately and efficiently to ensure straight pieces. Straighten the fabric by folding it in layers, selvedge to selvedge to fit on the cutting mat. Lay a triangle along the folded edge of the fabric and push it against the right side of the ruler until it is just at the edge.

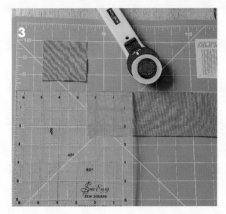

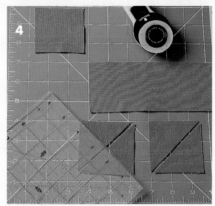

right sides together, so the marked seam line on the wrong side of the fabric is visible on both sides of the patchwork when sewing. Sew the seam through the pencilled lines with a short running stitch and occasional back stitch, using a single thread.

Begin and end each seam at the seam line (not at the edge of fabric) with two or three back stitches to secure the seam and sew from point to point, not edge to edge.

When joining the blocks and the rows together, do not sew the seam allowance down. Sew up to the dot marking the corner, then begin on the next side by taking a couple of extra small back stitches and continue sewing along the line. This leaves your options open as to which way to press the seam allowance when the block is completed.

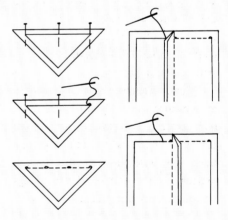

Hold the ruler down with your left hand, remove the triangle and begin cutting. Walk your hand up parallel with the cutter and continue to cut off the end of the fabric. Do not try to hold the ruler at the bottom as you will most likely move it.

Once you have straightened the fabric, use the cutter and ruler to cut strips of fabric to the width you require.

Squares, rectangles and triangles are all cut from strips. Remember when cutting squares and rectangles to add ½in to the desired finished measurement. For a 2in finished square cut a 2½in square. For a 2in x 4in finished rectangle, cut 2½in x 4½in.

Half square triangles are half a square with the short sides on the straight grain and the long side on the bias. To cut these triangles, cut a square in half diagonally. Cut the square ⅞in larger than the finished short side of the triangle to allow for seam allowances.

Quarter square triangles are used along the outside edge of a quilt

and some blocks are quarter square triangles. These triangles have their short sides on the bias and the long side on the straight grain. These triangles are cut from squares. Each square is cut into four on the diagonal and each is 1¼in larger than the finished long side of the triangle.

PIECING METHODS

Hand piecing

Pieces for hand piecing require precisely marked seam lines; marked cutting lines are optional. Place the template face down on the wrong side of the fabric and draw around it accurately with a sharp pencil. Leave space between patches for a ¼in seam allowance when cutting.

After marking the patches, cut outward from the seam line ¼in, measuring the distance by eye. Join the pieces

ENGLISH PAPER PIECING METHOD

This hand piecing technique involves basting fabric over a thin cardboard or paper template. The shapes are stitched together to form blocks and ultimately to form a quilt. Although time-consuming, this method results in precise, sharp seams and a professional finished appearance. It also has the advantage of being able to be picked up, put down and carried around.

When hand piecing over paper, cut out an exact sized light cardboard template for every pattern piece, as well as a cardboard pattern for every piece. Cut out the fabric shape using the cardboard pattern and include ¼in seam allowance all around.

Place the cardboard template in the centre of the wrong side of the fabric shape. Working one side at a time, fold over the seam allowance onto the template. Baste into place through the template, making sure the corners of the fabric are neatly folded in. For easy

removal of the basting, start with a knot and finish with a simple double stitch.

To join the patches together, place them right sides facing and match corners. With a matching thread, or a mid-grey thread which blends with most colours, join the edges from corner to corner using a tiny whip stitch and double stitch the corners. The stitch should be fairly small and not visible from the right side of the fabric. Make each block separately by sewing the smallest pieces together first to form units. Join smaller units to form larger ones until the block is complete. Press, then join the blocks together to form rows and the rows together to form the sampler or quilt top.

The cardboard templates can be removed when all the pieces are joined together. Turn the quilt over and press well with a warm iron and allow to cool. Then carefully remove the basting stitches and lift out each piece of cardboard separately.

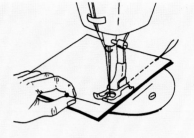

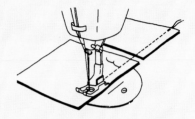

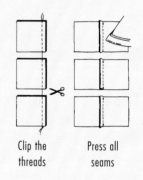

Clip the   Press all
threads   seams

1
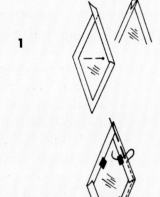

2
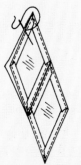

MACHINE PIECING

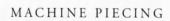

Accurate cutting is very important especially in machine piecing. Include seam allowances in the template and mark the cutting line on the back of the fabric.

Use white or neutral thread as light in colour as the lightest colour in the project. Use a dark neutral thread for piecing dark solids.

When machine sewing patches, align cut edges with the edge of the presser foot if it is ¼in wide. If not, place masking tape on the throat plate of the machine ¼in away from the needle to guide you in making ¼in seams. Sew along to the cut edge unless you are inserting a patch into an angle. Short seams need not be pinned unless matching is involved if the seam is long. Keep pins away from the

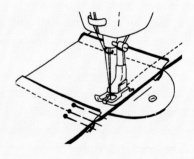

seam line. Sewing over pins is not good for sewing machine needles.

Use chain-piecing whenever possible to save time and thread. Sew one seam, but do not lift the presser foot. Do not take the piece out of the sewing machine and do not cut the thread. Instead, set up the next piece to be sewn and continue stitching. There will be small twists of thread between the two pieces. Sew all the seams you can at one time, then remove the 'chain'. Clip the threads, then press the seams.

When joining rows, make sure matching seam allowances are pressed in opposite directions to reduce bulk and make matching easier. Pin pieces together directly through stitching and to the right or left of the seam, removing the pins as you sew.

JOINING BLOCKS

Blocks joined edge to edge

Join the blocks to form strips the width of the quilt. Pin each seam very carefully, inserting a pin wherever seams meet, at right angles to the seam using a ¼in seam allowance. Join all blocks in the second row, continuing until all rows are completed. Press all seam allowances in the odd-numbered rows in one direction and all seam allowances in even-numbered rows in the opposite direction. When all rows are completed, pin two rows together so that seam lines match perfectly. Join rows in groups of two, then four, and so on until the top is completed. Press all allowances in one direction, either up or down.

Blocks joined with vertical and horizontal sashing

Join the blocks into strips with a vertical sash between each pair of blocks. Sew a horizontal piece of sashing to each strip, then join the strips to form the quilt top.

PRESSING

Press the seam allowances to one side, usually towards the darker fabric. Press quilt blocks flat and square with no puckers. To correct any problems in blocks, sashes or borders, remove a few stitches to ease puckers and re-sew.

APPLIQUE

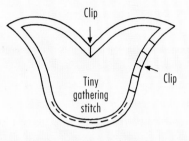

Diagram 1

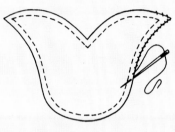

Diagram 2

Appliqué is not a difficult technique but basic rules do apply. Curved shapes should be smooth with no points, points should be a definite point, and there should be no puckers. Begin by marking around the template onto the right side of the fabric. Cut out the shape with a ¼in seam allowance. Turn the seam allowance under and baste. When there is a sharp curve sew a tiny running stitch just to the outside of the marked line. Gather slightly so that the curve sits well (see Diagram 1). Where there is a sharp point, mitre the corner as you are basting, and cut away any excess fabric. Be careful not to cut away too much. Pin the pieces to the background fabric making sure they are centred.

Cut a 15¾in length of thread and make a small knot. Make sure the knot sits underneath the piece being appliquéd, then bring the thread from the back through the background fabric and catch a couple of threads on the appliqué piece. When you begin to appliqué, make sure the needle enters the background fabric directly opposite

where it came out on the top piece and slightly under the piece being appliquéd (see Diagram 2). When you have completed stitching, finish off on the back with a couple of small back stitches.

ADDING MITRED BORDERS

Centre a border strip each side of the quilt top to extend equally at each end. Pin, baste, and sew strips in ¼in seams, beginning and ending at the seam line, not the outer edge of the fabric. At one corner, on the wrong side, smooth one border over the adjacent one and draw a diagonal line from the inner seam line to the point where the outer edges of the two borders cross. Reverse the two borders (the bottom one is now on top), and draw a diagonal line from the inner seam line to the point where the outer edges cross. Match the two pencil lines (fabrics right sides together), and sew through them. Cut away the excess, and press the allowances open. Repeat at the other corners of the quilt.

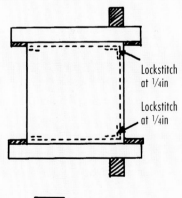

Lockstitch at ¼in

Lockstitch at ¼in

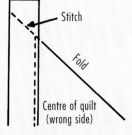

Stitch

Fold

Centre of quilt (wrong side)

There are many appliqué techniques which provide a range of different results. Here we present a few of them.

SHADOW APPLIQUE

The delicate muted effects that can be achieved with Shadow Appliqué are simple to work on clothes, cushions, quilts and wall-hangings.

Shapes are cut out of bright solid colour fabric, placed on a background, then covered with a transparent fabric such as voile or organdy. Small running stitches through the three layers hold the appliqués in position and create a subtle shadowing of the design.

The base fabric is traditionally white with strongly coloured appliqués, but a strong base with a matching transparent cover fabric can also highlight a pale contrasting design.

BRODERIE PERSE

Broderie Perse is the technique of cutting out motifs from printed fabrics and appliquéing them onto a plain fabric. While its name comes from its resemblance to Persian embroidery, its origins go back to the 18th century, and the use of brilliantly coloured fabric from India. The appliqué technique grew out of the necessity to conserve material and re-use the brilliantly coloured fabrics manufactured in India and imported to England. These durable cotton chintz fabric were prized for their bright, fast colours which contrasted with the drab English prints available at the time.

Featuring human figures, birds, animals, trees, flowers and vines with an Oriental flavour, the fabrics were imported by traders who felt that sales could be increased if they were printed to English tastes. The embroidery styles of the day were sent to India to be copied and the fabrics imported by the East India Trading Company. Sales were outstanding, but the livelihood of fabric manufacturers in Britain and France was seriously affected. The import of Indian chintzes was outlawed and use of the fabric banned on clothing, furniture or bed coverings.

The prized fabrics became scarce, and it was this that encouraged the popularity of Broderie Perse. Those who acquired small amounts of chintz cut the designs apart and appliquéd them to a larger piece of cloth to make them 'stretch' further. Used bed coverings and draperies were cut apart and the printed designs re-used as appliqués.

Three favourite styles of Broderie Perse emerged, with the most popular being the Tree of Life, another being an informal array of chintz cut-outs which covered the background in an all-over pattern; and the third featuring a central medallion with pieces organised within it.

When working Broderie Perse, the chintz fabric should be first washed to prevent shrinkage. The pieces for appliqué need careful selection, avoiding intricate pieces, as detail can be embroidered later.

Cut out the pieces with ¼in (6mm) seam allowance around all edges and clip the curves (see Diagram 1). Fold and baste the raw edges to the wrong side and press, or finish with slip stitching.

Arrange the chintz cut-outs on the background fabric, moving the pieces around for the most pleasing composition. Secure the pieces to the background using pins, basting stitches or a glue stick and slip stitch by hand or machine. Add fine details in embroidery (see Diagram 1).

Diagram 1
Clip the curved edges into the marked line, or the line of stay-stitching, but not beyond it.

HAND APPLIQUE

Before the advent of the sewing machine, all appliqué and quilting was done by hand, with some remarkable results.

Decide on the fabric and shape of your templates, then cut out your shapes. Stay stitch them to strengthen the edge of the fabric and allow it to roll under more easily. Clip any curved edges of each of each appliqué perpendicular to the marked outline or stay-stitching line (see Diagram 1). Clip just to the line, not beyond it. Straight edges do not need to be clipped. Make extra clips along deep curves for easier turning.

There are two different appliqué methods: the pre-baste technique which is used when exact placement of pieces is required; and the quicker needle-turn method which does not require basting (see Diagram 2).

If you are pre-basting your pieces, turn the raw edges ¼in (6mm) in to the wrong side and hand baste in place. Steam press the folded edges carefully. If you wish to have crisp edges or add stability to flimsy fabrics, cut iron-on interfacing to the size of the appliqué without seam allowances. Centre the

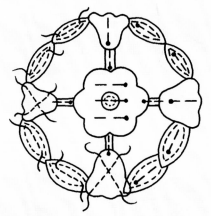

Diagram 2
The appliqués are secured to the background by pinning (right) and basting (left). On the left are the pre-basted appliqués. On the right are the unbasted appliqués, which overlap each other because of the seam allowances.

interfacing on the wrong side of the appliqué and press. Fold the seam allowances over the interfacing and baste.

For circles, use thin cardboard for a template. Work a round of basting stitches close to the raw edges of the circle appliqué, then place the template on the wrong side of the fabric. Pull the basting stitches, gathering the edges tightly around the template. Press gently, then pop out the template. Sew in place.

Cut fabrics for stems on the bias, adding ¼in (6mm) allowances to each. Cut thin cardboard templates to the required width and centre on the wrong side of the bias strip. Press the raw edges over the cardboard, then remove it. Shape the stem on the base using your fingers and steam.

Alternatively, you can cut a template to the exact shape of the stem. Centre the template on the wrong side of the bias strip and steam-press the edges gently over the template. Remove the template without distorting the stem and stitch it to the base. Always stitch the concave curves first.

Some people find it easier to prevent their appliqué from puckering if the work

is held taut in an embroidery hoop. Do not position the hoop over the piece you are sewing as it may distort the shape. Instead, centre the appliqué within the hoop.

Non-fraying fabrics such as felt, closely woven wool and leather do not need seam allowance. Sew these pieces to the base with stab stitches, worked about ⅛in (3mm) away from the raw edge in a line or worked just over the raw edge.

NEEDLE-TURN APPLIQUE

To appliqué using needle-turn, pin the appliqué piece in position on the right side of the base and turn the edges under as you are sewing the appliqué in place.

Use your fingertips to roll the seam allowance under. Turn it under just far enough to hide your pencilled outline or stay-stitching lines.

For curved or difficult areas, where your fingers may obstruct the view of your work, stroke the seam allowances underneath the appliqué using the tip and side of the needle.

Similarly, use the tip of the needle in all your work to ensure that the edges of the appliqués are smooth (see Diagram 3).

A little bit of practice will perfect the needle-turn technique.

When tackling wide corners, fold one edge of the appliqué ¼in (6mm) to the wrong side, then fold the second edge, similarly, overlapping the first. To appliqué the corner, again use the tip and side of the needle and the stroking technique to push the seam allowances beneath the appliqué (see Diagram 4).

For narrow corners the seam allowance needs to be trimmed and folded (see Diagram 5).

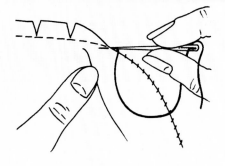

Diagram 3
For curved areas, use the side of your needle to stroke the seam allowances under the appliqué.

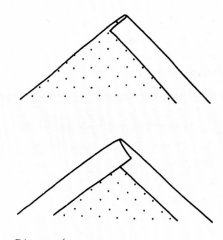

Diagram 4
For wide corners, fold one edge under first, then fold the second to overlap the first.

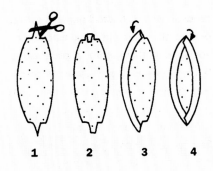

Diagram 5
If the corner is narrow, clip into the seam allowance ¼in (6mm) below the corner and trim to ⅛in (3mm); trim off the point just above the marked turning line (1). Fold down to the wrong side (2), then fold one edge of the appliqué ¼in (6mm) to the wrong side (3), fold the second edge similarly, overlapping the first (4).

When attempting sharp dips, commonly known as 'valleys' in appliqué, clip into the seam allowance to within a couple of threads of the outline or stay-stitching line.

Fold the raw edges to the wrong side. Ensuring that the seam allowances are separate, leaving virtually no fabric at the dip. Work close stitches at the dip to secure the raw edges and stop them fraying (see Diagram 6).

Diagram 6
Clip the seam allowance to the outline, in the valley, then fold the raw edges to the back, leaving almost no fabric at the dip. Work close stitches at the dip to secure the raw edges.

Decorative effects are a simple way to add a delicate finishing touch to a quilt. They can be achieved by working embroidery stitches on the appliqués, or by adding a variety of trims such as lace, beads, ribbon or Russian braid. To attach lace, position it exactly on the edge of the appliqué and secure it with running stitches in a matching coloured thread.

MACHINE APPLIQUE

Before starting, make sure your machine is in good working order, is clean and has a new needle fitted. Use cotton thread to match the appliqué and use an appliqué foot which has a wide space between the prongs and a groove on the underside, otherwise use a zigzag foot.

Cut the appliqué pieces out with no seam allowance and fuse lightweight interfacing or fabric stabiliser to the back of the background fabric. Arrange the appliqués in correct position on the base and secure with basting or a glue stick. Be sure to test the glue stick to ensure it will not permanently mark the fabric. Alternatively, secure the pieces using fusible webbing.

Using matching thread, stitch close to the edges of each appliqué using a medium length straight stitch. Sew slowly to prevent puckering. The appliqués should lie flat against the background.

Set the machine for a close zigzag or satin stitch and practise first on a scrap of similar fabric. The tension should be even and should not pull or make puckers.

Leave a long thread at the start and stitch along the edge of the appliqué, covering the raw edges.

The stitch width is dependent on the weight of the fabric. Use a thinner stitch for light fabrics and a wider stitch for heavier fabrics. A standard stitch width is about ⅛in (3mm).

Gently guide the fabric around the curves using a smooth movement, with-

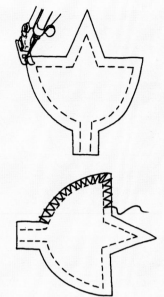

Diagram 7
To zigzag around corners, turn the fabric with the needle in the work, on the outside edge of the appliqué. The new line should overlap the end of the previous line.

out stopping, or having the stitches pile up on one another. Approach the corners slowly, zigzaging up to the outside edge of the appliqué and leaving the needle in the fabric on the outside edge. Raise the presser foot and turn the fabric, then lower the presser foot so the new line of zigzag overlaps the previous line (see Diagram 7).

Leave a long thread at the end. Thread the loose ends onto an embroidery needle and weave back through the zigzags.

Use the zigzag stitch to define shapes on the appliqué pieces, such as flower petals and veins on leaves.

Glossary

Adhesive/fusible webbing
Fibre material that is used to fuse two layers of fabric together when pressed with an iron (e.g. Vliesofix).

Appliqué
A piece of fabric that is hand sewn onto a background fabric with a running stitch, slip stitch or with embroidery stitches. It can also be attached with a zigzag machine stitch.

Backing
The bottom layer of a quilt sandwich. A piece of fabric the same size as the quilt top with approximately 2in extra allowance for take up.

Basting
Large hand or machine stitches which are used to hold a quilt sandwich together while it is being quilted.

Batting
Another name for wadding or padding.

Betweens
The name given to quilting needles. The shorter the needle, the higher the number.

Binding
A narrow strip of fabric used to finish off the edges of a quilt. Cut on the straight grain of fabric or on the bias. A binding can be made as a separate attachment, or by folding the backing over the top, or vice versa and stitching it, or by folding the edges of the top and backing inside, then sewing the folded edges together.

Blanket stitch
Decorative stitch suitable for both hand and machine work.

Border
The fabric around the outside of a quilt which can be wide or narrow, plain or pieced. Borders can give a finishing touch to a quilt and pull a design together. Many quilts, however, are made without borders.

Broderie Perse
A printed design fabric which is cut apart and sewn onto a background fabric as an appliqué.

Butting
Joining the ends of two pieces of fabric together.

Calico/muslin
A natural coloured plain-weave cotton fabric. Also known as muslin in America. Because of its hard wearing quality, it is almost always used as a quilt backing. Calico, in America, refers to a small floral patterned cotton fabric.

Chain stitch
Traditional hand embroidery stitch used to appliqué an outline and embellish a piece by hand.

Colourwash
A display of colours ranging from the lightest shade to the darkest.

Cross-cut
Cutting across intersecting rows.

Damask
A reversible fabric of linen, silk, cotton or wool, woven with patterns.

Dressmakers' carbon paper
Dressmakers' carbon paper has a special waxy finish on one side, and comes in a number of different colours. It is good for marking, or cutting lines on fabric. First test it on a piece of fabric to make sure that the marks will wash out. It is best to use carbon paper of a matching colour so that the marking is less noticeable.

Embroidery
The embellishment of fabric with surface stitching.

Felt
Felt is created by pressing the fibres of a non-woven fabric, such as wool, together with heat and moisture. Felt does not fray as it has no grain. It cannot be laundered.

Finger-press
Flattening the fabric between the thumb and forefinger, or creasing it into position with a fingernail.

Foundation
A base of lightweight fabric, interfacing or soft paper, on which patchwork or appliqué is sewn.

Four-patch quilt
A quilt made up of four large patchwork or appliqué blocks, usually surrounded by a border.

Grainline
The fibres or yarn in a piece of fabric as differentiated from the fabric itself. The grain of fabric should always run in the same direction on a quilt block, or on borders and sashings.

Homespun
Fabric similar in appearance to hand-spun or hand-woven fabric.

Medallion quilt
A large central motif surrounded by several different borders. Medallions can be used to quilt plain fabric blocks on a patchwork or appliqué quilt or as the central point of a single fabric quilt.

Nine-patch quilt
A quilt which is made up of nine patch-work or appliqué blocks, usually sur-rounded by a border.

Osnaburg
Coarse, even-weave cotton.

Overlay
To lay or place one piece of fabric on top of another.

Perlé Coton
A cotton embroidery thread that has a silky appearance. Available in a variety of colours and diameters. An excellent thread to use for embroidering crazy patchwork or for tying quilts.

Penny Rugg
Bed cover made from woollen scraps and decorated with floral motifs.

Polyfil
Trade name for loose stuffing used for filling cushions and soft toys. Also known as polyester fibrefill.

Puckering
Fabric sewn tightly or crookedly which gathers into wrinkles.

Puddle
Unquilted area between blocks.

Quilting frame
A four-sided frame which holds the three layers of a quilt tightly together to assist with even stitching.

Quilting stitch
A running stitch that is sewn through the quilt top, batting and backing to hold the three layers together. Quilting stitches can be worked in some form of design or at random.

Reducing glass
Used for viewing patchwork before it is sewn together to see how the finished design will look.

Reverse appliqué
The opposite of appliqué. A layer of fabric is removed to reveal the design.

Rod pocket
A seam sewn to hold a hanging rod.

Rotary cutter
A tool used to cut up to six layers of fabric at one time. The fabric is placed on a cutting mat and cut with a sharp circular blade which is drawn along the edge of a thick plastic ruler.

Rotary ruler
A thick clear plastic ruler printed with lines exactly $\frac{1}{4}$in apart. It is used with a rotary cutter. There are also diagonal lines indicating 45° and 60° marked on most rotary rulers.

Sampler quilt
A quilt made up blocks which are all different. Sampler quilts are used to teach different techniques.

Sawtooth border
Squares of fabric folded into triangles that are inserted into the edges of a quilt to finish it.

Selvedges
These are the finished edges of a piece of fabric. Selvedges should not be used in patchwork because the threads are woven more than the rest of the fabric and may shrink when the fabric is washed.

Templates
A pattern piece used to mark fabrics for patchwork, appliqué and quilting. Templates are usually made of strong cardboard or plastic. Templates can be kept and reused. A $\frac{1}{4}$in seam allowance should be added to each template.

Texture
The characteristic disposition of interwoven or intertwined threads which make up a textile fabric.

Tying
A quick way to hold the quilt sandwich together without using the traditional running stitches. The thread is inserted through the quilt at regular intervals and tied in a square knot or bow, or it can be secured with buttons.

Top
The top layer of a quilt sandwich made of patchwork, appliqué or one piece of fabric. The other two layers are made of batting and backing.

Wadding
Another term for batting/padding.

Warp
Vertical threads running through the length of a woven fabric.

Weft
The horizontal threads in a woven fabric.

Window template
The outline of the patchwork or appliqué shape with a $\frac{1}{4}$in seam allowance. The template appears as a window through which the fabric is seen.

Wool
A natural fibre woven from sheep's fleece. Woollen fabrics are warm, resilient and absorbent. Many early quilts were made from woollen fabrics.

Index

AUSTRALIAN COUNTRY CRAFT SERIES

The arrival of *Australian Country Craft & Decorating* magazine in 1991 signalled the beginning of a new era in craft in this country. The magazine's superb photographic features, polished editorial and meticulously researched projects have helped elevate craft from the relative obscurity of a cottage industry to the magnitude of a multi-million dollar industry.

Australian Country Craft & Decorating continues to raise the profile of craft and craftspeople in Australia. It has been the catalyst for a number of other craft publications and virtually all of them have been unbridled successes, none more so than *Australian Patchwork & Quilting*.

❖

Australian Patchwork & Quilting, together with the numerous quilting and applique specials it has inspired, is without doubt the leading magazine of its type in Australia. Locally, its popularity rivals that of *Australian Country Craft & Decorating* and it has gained a reputation overseas as a publication of quality and authority. Quite simply, if your interest lies in quilting, *Australian Patchwork & Quilting* magazine is essential reading.